HUMOR IN THE CLASSROOM

HUMOR IN THE CLASSROOM

From Busby to Brown

STEVEN E. DYCHE

Humor in the Classroom

Copyright © 2019 by Steven E. Dyche. All rights reserved.

No part of this publication may be reproduced, stored in a retrieval system or transmitted in any way by any means, electronic, mechanical, photocopy, recording or otherwise without the prior permission of the author except as provided by USA copyright law.

This novel is a work of fiction. Names, descriptions, entities, and incidents included in the story are products of the author's imagination. Any resemblance to actual persons, events, and entities is entirely coincidental.

The opinions expressed by the author are not necessarily those of URLink Print and Media.

1603 Capitol Ave., Suite 310 Cheyenne, Wyoming USA 82001
1-888-980-6523 | admin@urlinkpublishing.com

URLink Print and Media is committed to excellence in the publishing industry.

Book design copyright © 2019 by URLink Print and Media. All rights reserved.

Published in the United States of America
ISBN 978-1-64367-211-3 (Paperback)
ISBN 978-1-64367-210-6 (Digital)

1. Fiction
2. Education
3. Humor & Entertainment
22.01.19

Contents

Preface 7
Introduction 9

Chapter 1: Busby 13
Chapter 2: Senior High 16
Chapter 3: A College in South Dakota 28
Chapter 4: Higher Education in the Equality State 37
Chapter 5: Quasi College Administration—Down South 41
Chapter 6: Special ASU Students 48
Chapter 7: The Center 57
Chapter 8: The Math and Science Education Network 62
Chapter 9: Science Education at Brown University 69
Chapter 10: Some Special Colleagues 74
Chapter 11: Controversy 80
Chapter 12: Humor in Sports 83
Chapter 13: Campus Humor 96
Chapter 14: College Sports Humor 99
Chapter 15: Some Final Thoughts and Stories 106

PREFACE

◆

As the title of this book suggests, it is about humor in school. By school, I mean the larger, educational extension of the classroom and the building in which the classrooms are contained. I mean a larger more comprehensive definition of school: activities that take place in the auditorium, gymnasium, classroom, hallways, playground, and athletic fields. I mean everything that is related to learning brought about by teachers, coaches, administrators, and students themselves.

I have attempted to present this humor as it occurred chronologically in my life and to tie it to events that were important to me personally. I mention family members, friends, ball games, and historical events because it provides the setting for the humor. I make frequent mention of my athletic career primarily because it is such a rich source of humor. The book isn't intended to be about me, but revealing various events in my life were necessary in order for the reader to appreciate the humor. It may be the case that you had to be there! Some of the stories are more human interest than humorous.

All of the stories with the exception of the wrestlers in the introduction are true or are based on real situations. Some of the stories I found more heartwarming than hilarious, yet they have some bits of underlying humor in there somewhere. Sometimes being able to find the humor, even if in retrospect, is part of what made it important to me. Some names and situations have been changed out of deference to the participants. In many cases, just first or last names are used.

The vast majority of the humorous situations happened to me. A few of the stories are borrowed from educational colleagues. None are intended to be hurtful or cruel—only funny and amusing.

I wish to thank all of the students, teachers, administrators, and others who helped provide information for the book—either by design, or by unwittingly becoming part of one of the humorous incidents. I also thank Dixie Farthing and my daughter, Sherry Ceperich, for editing the manuscript and for their helpful suggestions concerning what content to include. Also, thanks to Chris Meadows and his suggestions for improving the manuscript.

INTRODUCTION

I come from a family of teachers and coaches—my dad, my uncle and several cousins on my father's side, and my cousin and two great aunts on my mother's side. I guess it was natural for me to become a teacher and to have a high interest in sports. One time in my early career I ran into Dr. Roland Renne, then President at Montana State College, in the Billings airport. I had known Dr. Renne since I was a kid—my aunt was his personal secretary for many years. When he asked me what I was doing, I replied that I was teaching Biology at Billings Senior High School. He responded, "Is that all you Dyches can do, is teach?" Although he said it jokingly, as I think back on it, I believe he was correct. I really think that teaching is the only profession in which I could ever attain even a modicum of success. Dr. Renne might have added, "Do you Dyches all have a sense of humor?" To that, I would also say, yes.

I grew up around humor, mostly puns and short, word-based jokes. My uncle told the story of his early one-room schoolhouse experience. Johnny and his sister both attended the school but were in different grades. One day Johnny got in trouble for getting mad at his sister and using some swear words. His punishment was to study the atlas and learn about some cities in Europe. After a time,

Johnny asked his teacher if Rotterdam was a bad word. "Why no," she said, "it is a large city in Holland."

"Good," the boy replied, "because sister just ate some of my candy and I hope it will rot her damn teeth out."

One time after school, two immigrant boys who were not overly familiar with the English language wanted to wrestle. "How long should we continue?" one boy asked. The other said, "Until one of us says 'Sufficient.'" They fought on and on—first one boy getting the advantage, then the other. It was almost dark when one boy finally shouted out, "Sufficient!" The other lad pounded the ground in anger. "I have been trying to think of that darn word for over an hour!" he cried.

School was always enjoyable for me. I liked having assignments, working on problems, reading about different people and countries. I also liked the academic calendar. It seems like there were plenty of vacations and time to play ball of some kind. Another reason I liked school was because I was good at it. (I emphasize *was* because in this day and age of technology, I fear I would not have done as well. Machines are difficult for me and I am buffaloed by modern technology.) Anyway, I was a good student and got a lot of attention from my teachers. I also became known as teacher's pet by some of my classmates. I remember sitting in my high school biology class thinking, "I would like to teach this class." I later found out that it was much tougher than it looked. I also discovered that humor can make the school day much more pleasant for both teacher and student and can actually help kids remember.

From that day as a high school sophomore, I wanted to be a teacher, preferably a biology teacher. When I was 15, a friend and I visited my uncle's house near a state university. He was a professor and had many textbooks—health, exercise science, botany and microbiology books. That same year I was taking high school biology, which I loved. I also liked and admired the teacher. So I guess I was hooked.

I entered college, not at the university where my uncle taught, but at a small private school not too far from home, ostensibly on an athletic scholarship. My freshman year I enjoyed the academics and a cheerleader girlfriend more than the athletic competition. So I dropped the sports, although I continued to go to games of all kinds, coaching and refereeing from the stands, never making a mistake.

As a college freshman I can remember being in a zoology lab one afternoon. We were using the microscope to observe protozoans. I also recall that there was a soft snow falling. I was very engrossed in the observations of these unicellular creatures, so engrossed that my professor came by and gently shook me by the arm. "Mr. Steve," he said, "the lab has been over for nearly two hours. I have to leave now but you may stay. Just turn out the lights when you leave." I literally got lost in time observing the unicellular beings. I loved watching those microscopic creatures—numerous and varied as they were.

The first practical challenge regarding my future career was student teaching during my senior year in college. Could I really teach? Turns out I practice taught in the same high school and classroom where I would later teach for 12 years. I had a good experience although my supervising teacher's wife died during my semester at the school, so I sort of had to go it alone. I got along OK, but possibly could have learned more in a different situation. During this time I met a Mr. Bill to whom I will refer later, and some other biology teachers and a lot of great kids.

CHAPTER 1

◆

Busby

After a stint at graduate school (M. Ed.) and marriage to my longtime sweetheart, I was ready to get out in the real world. Unfortunately, I finished my graduate degree at the state university at mid-year so it was tough finding a job. I managed a position teaching eighth grade on the Cheyenne Indian Reservation—a boarding school operated by the Bureau of Indian Affairs located in Busby, Montana. The school was unique in that it housed Native American (at that time, the term Native American was not yet in use) students from various Indian tribes around the state—kids who had been abandoned, had a scrape with the law, had lost one or more parents, etc. The school also welcomed local kids who were not boarders, some of whom were non-Indian. It made for a different mix—a lot of excitement and some behavior problems.

We moved to the reservation in the dead of winter. Adding to the confusion, our daughter decided to be born just as we were preparing to move. We had some very nice economical housing—rent was $18 a month; a real bargain, even in 1964. The town consisted of a single general store including filling station and post office. On Wednesday nights, movies were shown at the high school, a swinging place no doubt! Mrs. D. about went nuts, and for good reason, being a new mother and a social person with few outlets in this tiny town. Still, it was a job—a challenge I was up to meeting, or so I thought.

The school year was an eye opener. With a few exceptions most of the 8th graders performed below grade level. For some, English was a second language; others were just slow. Most of the kids, primarily the Native American children, had a great sense of humor and usually could laugh at themselves. Sometimes feuds would break out among the Indian children representing different Native American tribes. Occasionally, long forgotten hostilities would bubble to the surface in the form of traded insults, sarcastic remarks about another tribe, or even some physical contact. Mostly, the incidents were short lived and soon forgotten, but they never ceased to surprise me when they popped up.

Teaching in Busby provided for some humorous anecdotes; here are a few that I remember.

A rather precocious female Blackfoot Native American girl asked me about the title of a book she wanted to read. "What is this book *Candy Stripers* about?" (But she pronounced it "strippers".) When I told her it involved young women volunteering to help at hospitals she said, "Oh, I guess I don't want to read it then." She obviously was hoping for something a bit more racy. Her favorite saying when she wanted to leave class was, "Let's bug jazz out of here." I still say it today when I become impatient! Once when I asked the class during an oral quiz to name the largest country in South America, she wildly raised her hand and shouted out, "I know this one, it is Brassiere."

At the graduation in May, a well-known Native American speaker and educator from the Southwest told the story of an earlier graduation attended by the grandparents of one of the graduates. That speaker went on about Cum Laude, Summa Cum Laude, and other Latin words ad nauseam. Finally the grandmother said to the grandfather, "What he say?" The grandfather turned to her and said, "I think he say, 'school is out'."

On a field trip to a local town to purchase clothing for all of the 8th graders, the same Blackfoot girl who had wondered about *Candy Stripers* asked me what the road sign, "No Driving on Shoulder" meant. When I told her that drivers were to stay in their lanes and not to drift over to the road edge, she replied that this didn't sound as exciting as she thought.

Some of the Indian students had nicknames. I often wondered about Native American birth names and asked frequently if they used nicknames. I found out one day when I intercepted a note written to a young lady with the last name of Little Whirlwind. The note was addressed to Baby Tornado. I found that to be quite clever.

We left Busby on a rainy June day never to return, but thankful for the experience. A few days earlier, I received a contract to teach biology at Billings Senior High—the very school where I had practice taught a couple of years earlier. We were very excited about the impending move, Dona even more so than I.

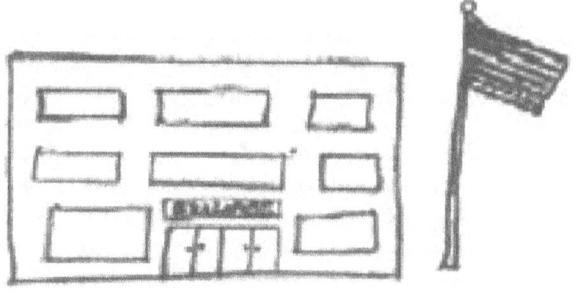

CHAPTER 2

◆

Senior High

The following dozen years I taught at a large city high school in Montana's largest town. I had student-taught there and liked the population mix that included students who were Hispanic, Native American, African American, Caucasian, children of farmers and ranchers, middle class kids, and kids from the town's "old money" families. Some of the humor at the high school came from my own ineptness and I literally brought some things on myself. One day I was telling the class about hookworms and other parasitic diseases. I was quite excited as the class seemed so interested. I wanted to say the tiny worms burrow up through the soles of your feet but my words got mixed and came out as "through the folds in your seat." The rest of the period was lost.

A not-so-humorous situation occurred one day during an introductory lab exercise that required using the microscope. I told students to look through the scope with their left eye but to keep their right eye open to help see what they were drawing. In this case it was cells. When I looked at a young lady's drawing (she was Polish, her parents couldn't speak English, and Sophie, although very bright, wasn't used to the nuances of the English language as I found out later), I asked, "What in the heck is that?" She said, "Well, it is a triangle." I responded that I didn't recognize any triangular shaped protozoans and jokingly added that it was the ugliest thing I had seen in my life. I moved on to help some other students when someone tapped me on the shoulder.

"Sophie is crying, Mr. D."

"Is she hurt?" I asked.

Her lab partner said, "Only her feelings from what you said about her drawing!" This was a lesson learned not to say heartless things to students, even in jest.

Another girl in a different class that was conducting the same activity was writing with her left hand. I kiddingly suggested that she was using the wrong hand. She said, "Mr. D., I can use any hand I feel like using."

I said, "Oh yes, I know, I was only joking".

She responded, "Yes, I know—but I can use either hand. Let me show you." She proceeded to write halfway across her paper with her left hand, then switched the pencil to her right hand and continued writing her sentence. I couldn't discern where the left hand stopped and the right hand began. Talk about being ambidextrous!

Still another student, another year, but carrying out the same assignment, was using her right eye but writing with her right hand. When I advised her that she should use her left eye, she told me that she couldn't use her left eye and see anything. I told her to please try. She responded that it wouldn't do any good. I again said please. She remained firm with a no. Finally, I asked, "Why not?" She came back with, "Because my left eye is glass." I was not so particular about which eye a student used at the microscope after that humiliating episode.

Another memorable incident, although not humorous at the time, took place during my last year at the school. We were doing some work with individualized instruction and two of my students were in the resource room next door. That room was also staffed by a certified biology teacher. I remembered that the students would need some information in order to finish the lab assignment. I erringly left my classroom for only a few short minutes. When I left, all of the students seemed to be busy and on task, but when I returned, bedlam was occurring. There was clay stuck to the blackboards, apparently thrown there at a very high velocity. Students were standing in their chairs, many of them yelling at the top of their voices, and it appeared that the room had just been hit by a hurricane. Yes, this was my last period class—large but usually attentive and well behaved, despite having to meet late in the day. I had left the room briefly before and nothing out of the ordinary had occurred, but on this day all heck had broken loose. Something in me snapped and in a loud voice I announced to the class that during my teaching career I had taught a murderer, two rapists, an armed robber, and kids that couldn't spell "cat" when spotted the "c" and the "a", but I had never in my entire teaching career witnessed such a display of outright disregard for rules and decorum. I told them they were a bunch of untrained, poorly behaved savages and that I was going back to the Resource Room for three minutes and when I returned, the room had damn well (one of my few cusses as an educator) better be clean. When I returned in a bit more than three minutes you could hear the proverbial pin drop, and the room was spic and span. I had never seen it so clean. How they were able to right that room, which only minutes before had looked like the remnant of a weather disaster, I'll never know. I often have wondered why we couldn't utilize the energy of 30 high school sophomores to do all kinds of work using short bursts of their limitless energy. The custodian had no work to do that night in Room 301. I am sure he went home wondering what happened to that normally messy biology teacher and class. He probably thought we were gone on a field trip or something.

Speaking of crimes, I did have a student who was arrested and was found guilty of murder. It was sensationalized in the local papers; the victim was a well-known athletic figure. The kid involved had been a quiet, uninterested student that, in retrospect, I had not made an effort to engage. I always wondered if I had taken more interest in him and provided a bit more direction and guidance that things would have been different. He was sentenced to life in prison. I doubt that the little formal biology knowledge I tried to force down his throat is doing him much good these days.

Another student, this time a minority male who was a borderline student at best, was working away on a lab activity when the assistant principal and two cops came into the room, grabbed the boy, and handcuffed him. I don't remember them reading him the Miranda Act—but it may have been previous to the existence of that bit of legal protection. As the boy was being hauled out of class, he shouted that no one was nice to him. I volunteered that I tried to be.

"Well, maybe you was OK to me," he countered; little solace for the situation. As an after-thought, I ran out of the room with the boy's biology book.

"Hey, you forgot this," I said.

"Forget it, he won't need it where he's going," commented the officer. We never heard about the boy or his fate. I am willing to wager that had he not been a member of a minority, he might have been treated with more civility.

In my early years of teaching, I was proud of my ability to call former and present students by name. Kids seemed to like this but it didn't continue as the years passed by. I eventually got some names mixed up and called Mary Smith "Jane Smith" and frequently called younger brothers and sisters by their older sibling's names. One such situation was a cause of some real consternation to me for most of an academic year. One source of the problem may have been my seating charts that basically were arranged alphabetically. A student who I will call George sat in the first seat on the right-hand side of the room in row one. George was a mature, polite kid and an A-/B+ student. Two years later, his brother Bill sat in the same seat. Although the boys sort of looked alike, there was not much similarity between them other than the fact that they shared the same last name. I don't believe Bill passed an exam the entire semester.

Unfortunately, I fell into the habit of calling Bill, "George." He would get very angry at this, and try as I might, I still sometimes slipped. A habit of Bill's was to come into class early and slam his books down on his desk so that it could be heard halfway down the hall. Even though I asked him not to do it, he still persisted. Bill never raised his hand in class and when called upon, he seldom tried to answer a question. One day during lab, Bill was standing at his lab station, drawing on the wall. I became furious and advised him that he was about to flunk, which could lead to him dropping out of school, and in a year or so, he would be draft eligible and sent to Viet Nam and possibly killed. His comment: "That would beat being in here." A subtle clue that he didn't like my class much. I was at my wit's end about what I might do to turn Bill around. Then one morning during home room announcements, I heard a voice say that the intramural basketball championship was to be played that night and that Bill was among the players listed on one of the contending teams. When Bill walked into class later that day and had once again slammed his books to the desk, I asked what time the game was to be played. Of course, he played dumb and responded with, "What game?" Finally, he asked if I liked basketball and I said I did. He said, "You weren't any good, were you?" I was able to answer that I had played in high school and one year of college ball. I did attend the game that night, and Bill's team won; he was one of the best players on the court. The next day, again after another book slamming episode, I congratulated him. He didn't say much, but I thought I detected a small smile.

That weekend I attended the high school varsity basketball team game and for some reason I was by myself. During the first quarter I felt a presence beside me. When I looked to see who it was, I about fell out of my seat! Yes, it was Bill. About the only thing he said was that "we ought to beat these guys." A few minutes later he was gone.

I'm not going to say that Bill became an A student after that, but he did pass the class. He mostly stopped slamming his books on the desk when he came in, and the few times that he forgot he said, "Sorry." When I now called on Bill he attempted an answer, even though his explanations often were incorrect. He even raised his hand a couple of times, but once it was to ask to leave the room. Still, progress was made with one of my most difficult students. I had been told by my coaches that playing basketball would pay off some day in ways that I didn't expect. In this case, it certainly was true.

HUMOR IN THE CLASSROOM

Speaking of names, I often taught a biology section that was geared for slower learners. I enjoyed working with these kids; most tried hard and appreciated my efforts to help them. During the first day of class I would pass the seating charts around the room so students could determine if I had spelled their names correctly, if they were in the right seat, and so they might know the names of some of their classmates. One time a young woman named Margaret said, "No, this isn't right—I told you I wanted to be called Peaches." Even the slowest class members seemed to wonder why.

Sometime about my seventh or eighth year at Senior, a rather flirtatious female student told me she was going to be out of school for a few days, having an operation. I asked about the cause and she replied that she was having her tail removed. It seems that she was born with the rudiments of a tail attached to her coccyx. She wanted to know if she could bring the dismembered appendage with her when she came back to school. I was a bit indefinite in my response and never did see the tail. A few years later while lecturing about the role of lysosomes in the cells and how they sometimes break and their enzymes dissolve cells, I remembered this story about the young lady's tail and pointed out how the lysosomes had failed in this case. A male student raised his hand and asked if the tail had fur on it. I was so flustered I could only respond, "I am not sure."

I worked with some very interesting colleagues. Mr. B. (sometimes called Wild B.) was a former coach and jock and had a very short fuse. One time, another colleague, Mr. R., and I were in the lab prep room situated between the two classrooms but with access to both rooms. We heard a disturbance in Wild B.'s room so we quietly tried to peek in. Just then, Mr. B hollered "If you do that again I'll break your g.d. neck!" Mr. R. and I evidently were not as well concealed as we would have liked. When Mr. B. looked up he saw us peeking through the partially open door—"And I'll break your necks too if you don't get the hell out of here, now!" he shouted as he glared at us. Mr. R. was larger than I, and that day he was also quicker, as he beat me to the other door leading back to his room. I guess we wanted to snoop but didn't have the guts to stay. I am not saying we were afraid of Mr. B., although one time when he was coaching football, he broke an assistant coach's arm. (He probably referred to breaking his "g.d." arm when it happened.) Another time, Mr. B. lifted a 60 gallon fish tank, mostly filled with water, all by himself. Mr. R. and I beat a hasty retreat and silently admitted that discretion was the better part of valor—at least at that moment.

Looking back over 30 years and all things considered, I really believe that my biology teaching colleagues were basically good hearted and well schooled in biology. They gave me, the novice, a lot of good teaching advice and modeled some excellent teaching—the neck breaking threat not withstanding.

Another incident at the high school involved the Biology Department's pet snake, Bob. Each morning before class, a student or two would come by and get the garter snake out of its cage and play with it. One morning the "old school" typing teacher from across the hall went ballistic when she saw the docile reptile: "I don't ever want to see that thing in my room, do you understand me?" That probably was the wrong thing to say to a small group of boys, a couple of whom didn't like the woman anyway. One morning a couple of weeks later I heard a blood curdling scream, and Ms. Typing Teacher bug jazzed out of the room at top speed. She didn't come back that day or next. As I found out second hand, one of the boys had "borrowed" the snake without permission and placed it under the cover of her demonstration typewriter. When Ms. Old Fashioned Typing Teacher took off the cover to begin her typing lesson, she saw Bob, and stuff hit the proverbial fan. The biology faculty were called in and dressed down by the principal and an apology note was drafted. Bob was no longer to be allowed out of his cage. A humorous story now, and then too, maybe, but definitely not to either the typing teacher or the principal. The boys and I still thought Ms. Old Fashioned brought it on herself.

In a somewhat related reptile class pet story, a teacher colleague, Ms. Sinclair, while teaching science in Florida during the late 1970s, had a land tortoise that was kept in a terrarium at the back of the classroom. One day, Ms. S. noticed that the pet reptile was missing. In its place was a ransom note saying she could get the animal back if she placed $10 in the terrarium before tomorrow morning. She told her class that there would be no ransom money paid, but there would be some low grades given to some likely suspects unless the pet was returned unharmed by class time the next day. Sure enough, the next morning she found the tortoise in its home—only it had been painted with psychedelic colors with the word "Benji" on the side to resemble the cartoon Volkswagon Beetle, a popular icon of the era. Reptiles in the classroom may be too much temptation for some youngsters prone to pulling pranks.

An older and somewhat eccentric chemistry teacher had his students abuzz by his actions at the class demonstration desk one winter morning. The teacher, Mr. D., who was a bit of a slob at best, had been at the demo desk leaning over to pick up a lab item. When he bent over his tie got caught in a desk drawer; for some reason Mr. D. dropped the drawer key as he closed the now-locked drawer. There he was, facing the class, bent over the desk and turning purple in the face as his tie began choking him. Instead of asking a student for assistance in unlocking the drawer, he picked up a pair of scissors off the desk and reached down and released himself by cutting his tie in half. Mr. D. was known for his eccentricities but this was almost too much, even for the students.

The gathering place for faculty members was, of course, the Teacher's Lounge. In my earlier years at the school, I didn't go in there much—too smoky, but as the years went by, folks stopped smoking so much and the air sort of cleared out. I would occasionally peek in the door and if the Lounge was being frequented by mostly non-smokers, I would pop in for a while. I mostly listened and added little to fuel the conversation fire. A new face in the lounge was that of the recently hired choral music teacher. The previous guy, although very good, had been something of a loner and didn't identify well with other faculty. The new guy, Mr. H., was into sports, storytelling, chatting—more of a man's man. He came to us from another town where the school superintendent was a bit notorious and known to be difficult. One noon my teacher friend, Mr. R., asked the music man, "What kind of a guy was Superintendent Mr. X anyway?" Mr. H. responded, "He was a real Prince." Mr. R. looked surprised and then the musician added, "A real prince, p-r-i-c-k, prince". The entire lounge broke into applause.

Some days the lounge was fertile ground for jokes—never about students, but just jokes that helped ease typical job stress. The master joke teller was an art teacher named Mr. L. He would get into the appropriate accent (if required) and made the jokes come alive. One story involved three new U.S. immigrants from Italy. One night they were talking about which Italian woman they would like to take on a date. The first guy suggested Gina Lollobrigida; she is beautiful and what a figure. The second fellow thought he preferred Sophia Loren for much the same reason. The third guy said, although he didn't know much about her, he would like Virginia (and what sounded like) Peepoleenie. "Who the heck is that?" the first two guys asked. "I dunno, all I know is what I read in the morning paper," the third guy added. He proceeded to get the newspaper out and opened it to the front page. The headline read: "State to Hire 500 Men to Lay Virginia Pipeline." "That Peepoleenie woman must be something," the third guy mused. I laughed so hard I about fell out of my chair. In fact, when I went up to my room for the next class, I listed on the absence sheet for that period the name Virginia Pipeline. I was soon visited by a couple of student helpers who said that they looked through all the records and could not find that student. "I think she just enrolled," I weakly replied; however, when the principal found out about my little shenanigans, he was not pleased, even though he had laughed at the story Mr. L. had told. I thought it was worth it.

Teaching at this large, almost inner-city type school was the most fulfilling academic experience of my life. The kids were, for the most part, easy to be around and many were very bright. I will always remember a two-person lab team, females who both had top-notch science fair projects. Later, one went to MIT, the other to Harvard. My colleagues were superb; I learned so much from them, and the administrators were solid and very supportive. The school was not only the biggest in the state, it was, in my opinion, the best of Montana's several hundred high schools. My next to last year there, Billings Senior High was named the winner of the Bellamy Award—national recognition for distinction.

After seven years of teaching at the high school, I was offered a one-year sabbatical to work on a doctorate degree. The stipulation was that I return to the high school to teach for a minimum of two years after the leave was completed. We had recently moved into our first house and, although we now had a daughter and a son, my wife and I decided to go back to Missoula. We had spent the previous four summers there while I worked on my M.S. degree. It turned out to have been a good decision as all four family members had positive experiences that year.

The year after I returned to Senior High from my sabbatical, I had a red—haired kid in class who sat in the back row and didn't say boo. At the end of the first grading period when I added up his points it appeared that he had earned an A. I double-checked to be sure. I definitely didn't think he was A student material, but there it was. He received an A each marking period and by the end of the year did manage a few words in class. I carefully watched him during lab periods and he was very thorough and quite reflective; yet I wasn't convinced about his abilities. I sort of forgot about him; he wasn't the type you would remember. One afternoon two years later he came by my classroom after school. He asked if I would do him a favor. I replied I would but was stunned to find out the request was for a letter of recommendation to Johns Hopkins

University. I thought, "Who the heck does this guy think he is? He'd do well just to get into Montana State". Sure enough, he informed me before school ended that year that he had been accepted at Hopkins. One evening a few years later my wife asked me to go to the convenience store for some item or another. While there, I bumped into the red-headed kid and a couple of his buddies. I asked him what he was doing and he told me he was home from a break at Johns Hopkins Medical School—as were his two friends. After I congratulated him he said, "Mr. D. there is something I have wanted to tell you."

"What is that?" I asked impatiently.

"Well sir, you are the best teacher I ever had." I told him he must have had some terrible instructors over the years, but I am sure from the tears in my eyes that he knew I appreciated his comments.

But in a sense I was right all along—the comment he made like the one above was proof the kid couldn't have been too bright, MD that he is now!

At the other end of the academic spectrum, I remember a young lady who was preparing her required biology research project. These generally ran the gamut from outstanding to respectable to god-awful. For example, the two girls who went, respectively, to MIT and Harvard had projects on animal and plant products which could be used in lieu of anti A and anti B serums in human blood typing and inducing carcinogenic tumors into plants, then dissipating those tumors with natural products. The project submitted by this young lady was not quite of that quality. She wanted to know the effect of certain environmental factors on two types of eggs—chicken and rabbit. Something was not quite right with the project. Had I not talked about the reproductive differences between birds and mammals? Sometimes one really has to wonder if his efforts have made any impact at all.

A fun, non-teaching assignment that I drew each year was recording the statistics at the high school football games with my friend Larry. We both liked sports and felt like we were making a real contribution to our team. Coach A. helped make us feel important as well. Sitting in an enclosed booth was a real bonus on a cold Montana fall evening. It was an even bigger bonus if it happened to be raining or snowing. After the game, we took the final stats down to the locker room of the winning and losing coaches. Seems like I had my share of taking stats to losing coaches who oftentimes were in no mood to receive some "stat guy."

One night when we were playing our cross-town rivals, the West High Bears, we were literally kicked out of our booth by the West announcer. He claimed he had a "hold" on that booth. So our "digs" for the big game were not so good. We could overhear the announcer during the game. Boy, was he biased. He would say things like, "The Bear's runner is in the clear, look at him go—hmmm, no gain." Or, "The Bears runner is all the way up to the 42 yard line, fourth down and still 10 yards to go." So, for a little payback we started copying the announcer, saying in loud voices, "Look at him go—no gain." It was easy enough for us to mock him that game as the Senior Broncs won handily and we had a bunch of Senior High fans to protect us. We did hear some comments as the announcer was leaving about Senior's faculty members being poor sports.

In the fall of 1975, contract talks between the Billings School Board and the Billings Chapter of the NEA came to an impasse and teachers went on strike. The work stoppage went on for over three weeks and teachers missed 17 days of teaching for which we were not paid. This pay cut put a severe crimp in a lot of pocket books. Hotheads on both sides of the question added fuel to the fire. I personally voted not to strike; however, as a member of the NEA, I felt it incumbent on me to follow the organization's majority vote. Additionally, I thought the School Board was not playing fair and 35 years later, I still don't think they were. The Board spent thousands of dollars to hire a strike negotiator (money that could have gone for salaries, books, materials, etc.). Plus, they wanted every dispute settled in their favor and left no room to negotiate. The only humorous item that I remember about the strike was the placard I was carrying. It read: School Board says, "Teachers, lower your demands." Teachers say, "School Board, Up yours." Nothing else seemed laughable during those tough three weeks. When the strike was finally settled in late October, there were some permanently hurt feelings, some marriage break-ups and cracks in what I had believed was Montana's finest school system. After the strike ended, I dusted off my resume (why was I teaching at a high school with a doctorate degree, anyway?). I vowed I would get out if I could, and see if I could find another job that would still fit the needs of my wife and family. Actually, the remaining portion of the school year went fairly smoothly for me. I had some great kids that year. Even during the strike they sent me notes telling me they missed me and loved me. I wrote back with similar messages. It turned out that I did get another job—this time at the collegiate level in a neighboring state. So, I left Billings Senior, but not without shedding a tear. It was a great school, despite the trauma during my last year there.

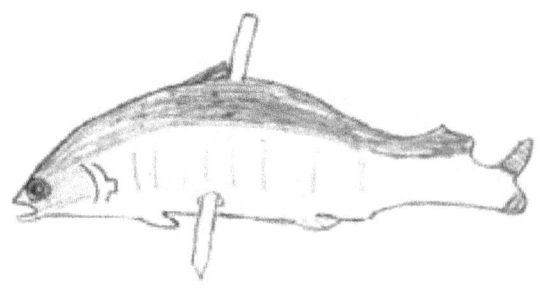

CHAPTER 3

◆

A College in South Dakota

After 12 years of teaching high school biology in Montana's largest city, my wife and I decided that we would take a college teaching job in Spearfish, South Dakota. I would supervise student teachers and teach some education courses. So leaving some wonderful friends behind, we left Billings for good. I think my wife hated moving more than any of us, although our son had a tough school adjustment. Nevertheless, I felt the support of the entire family in my next academic venture at Black Hills State College. Finally, a teaching position in higher education—my dream come true. I had earned a doctorate degree after the sabbatical from high school. I also previously completed a second master's degree after several summers of course work. The move would only be a six-hour drive and I thought we still could maintain our associations with our friends in Billings. Although we did go back a few times, basically our Montana relationships would become dimmer and dimmer and finally almost completely flicker out. My own family in the state was becoming older and was beginning to die out. Dona's family had moved to Colorado. Today, only my elderly mom and a sweetheart of a cousin remain. I do visit my old basketball coach when I can. During my first year at Black Hills State, I worked in the Education Department with the supervision of student teachers being my primary duties; however, I soon missed teaching science, and when a science educator position opened up at the college the next year I applied for it. The gods were with me and I landed the job.

Most of my responsibilities were in the area of science education and biology. One summer when working with primary grade teachers, I recall an elderly, grandmother-type first grade teacher. She was from North Dakota and was at our school for some summer in-service. I know she meant well and loved kids, but she was not the sharpest tool in the shed. She once demonstrated a unit on weather that overall sounded fairly decent, but I knew from having her in a measurement class that she did not understand the concept of negative numbers. One of the activities for her children was to take the daily temperature, both in the morning and in the afternoon. I asked her about the temperature results, knowing that it gets very cold in ND and that she didn't understand negative numbers. I asked what she did on the days that were below zero. She responded, "Well, we don't take the temperature on those days." Wow, I thought, that certainly wipes out most of January and February. She was such a nice person, but I frequently gave a silent prayer of thanks that she was not going to teach my children or my grandchildren.

Then there was Estes, a Native American male enrolled in our Science for Elementary Teachers class. The day before the final exam, Estes dropped by to tell me his wife was in the hospital and he was afraid he wouldn't have much time to study. I pointed out that the exam was hands-on and wouldn't involve a lot of rote memorization. If he could just demonstrate the science processes we had so diligently covered, I thought he would be OK. The next morning at exam time—no Estes. About twenty minutes into the exam period, here he came, unshaven and wearing colored glasses. He said he was sorry he was late, and could he take the test? I skeptically gave him a copy of the exam with directions. He sat looking at it for maybe 10 minutes, then gave the exam back to me.

"I cannot take the test today," he proclaimed. "Why not?" I asked.

"Because I am drunk," he countered.

I was a bit exasperated but told him to come back tomorrow and take the exam then. That afternoon I received a call from the campus Ombudsman asking if Estes and I had words. I apprised him of the situation and added that since Estes had seen the exam (sort of) that I would have to deduct 10 points from his score. He thought that was fair. The next morning Estes did arrive on time to take the final exam. He worked away on it for a while but left without completing all of the tasks. When I scored his test, I found that he only made 10 points. Remembering to deduct the 10 points I had mentioned to the Ombudsman, Estes wound up with a score of 0. Although I was agitated by the whole sordid story, my wife, mom, and mother-in-law all found it humorous in an ironic sort of way. I guess you would have had to have been there!

Yearly student evaluations of faculty were another source of humor, or at least they were at times. Most students were fairly kind with their ratings and remarks although I received a few negative stingers. One said I was a bad teacher, another said they were looking forward to taking other science classes because I wouldn't be teaching them. One guy, who for some reason signed his name, wrote, "Let Dyche teach here until he is dead." I wasn't sure if that was a positive or negative remark.

One year I had a couple of African students in class who had been trained in their country to stand up when addressing a faculty member. One day I was demonstrating osmosis using a dialysis baggie, starch, and iodine. I brought the apparatus over to where one of the African boys was sitting so he could see things better. I was immediately in front of his seat and asked him a question, forgetting his standing up habit. When he jumped up to answer me, he of course hit the baggie-starch-iodine apparatus and iodine flew all over my beige (now purple) tie. We were both embarrassed by our clumsiness, but the class found it comical. A couple of kids even thought we had planned it to sort of relax the class. Not so, but most students got the answer right on a test question involving osmosis through a dialysis baggie.

During an elementary teacher's math/science workshop, participants were assigned the task of obtaining the circumference and diameter of a particular tree. Each pair of teachers had their own assigned tree. Participants were given string and meter sticks to make their determinations. They were also asked to find the relationship between the circumference and the diameter. The first team to report stated that the circumference of their tree was a little over three times the diameter of their rather large tree. A second group measured a much smaller tree. They stated that the circumference also was about three times bigger than the diameter of their tree, but added that the measurements must not have been correct since they had a small tree and got the same answer as the team that measured the large tree. I originally thought my well-planned lesson on pi had been for naught, but on the unit exam most students remembered the humorous tree measuring activity and got the questions pertaining to circumference/diameter correct.

Once, at a workshop, we took the teachers to an orchard of tall trees interspersed with large boulders. Our point was to get the teachers to make inferences about the oldest thing in the orchard and to give reasons why. More than one participant listed the two instructors as the oldest objects in the orchard because they had gray hair, were balding, and had wrinkles. We responded that we had been told that we were older than the hills, but never older than giant trees, huge boulders, and dirt.

Often my summer workshops for elementary teachers were, not surprisingly, filled entirely by women. One time during such a workshop on identifying plants, we were walking over some hilly terrain. We came to a place where we needed to jump over a small ditch. As I feared, one teacher slipped and twisted her ankle. As the only male in the group I took on the persona of an athletic trainer/medical doctor. I examined her injured limb and loudly stated that it was swollen, blue, and the ugliest ankle injury I had ever seen. The teacher, between low moans, kept saying, "Dr. D., Dr. D." and I kept telling her to try to relax and keep quiet.

Again she said, "Dr. D., Dr. D." and I abruptly shouted, "What is it?"

She replied, "You are examining the wrong ankle." I wanted to crawl into that ditch and hide my red face and bruised ego for an eternity.

One semester I was teaching a large section of introductory biology. A few of our college's clientele were nontraditional types, often from a nearby air base or were dependent spouses of military personnel. That year, I had two very intelligent, very motivated, attractive women in their early 30's competing for top honors in the class. One was brunette, whom I'll call Tina, and the other a blonde that I will name Leigh. They were friends—off the field of battle—and were also lab partners. Both put hours into their studies and I believe there was a bit of rivalry over the professor's attention as well. Each spent considerable time going over with Dr. D. material that they already knew very well. To make a point of how picky they would be in answering test questions, let me refer to a genetics question on a biology exam. Students were to choose the answer that reflected observable traits in a human. I had indicated "tall, dark and handsome" as the best response, but they argued for the answer "none of the above" because handsome was not really an observable trait—that it was in the eye of the beholder. They had me on a technicality so I grudgingly gave them credit but was steamed that the two of them had outsmarted me. They were probably sitting outside in Leigh's van laughing at me at that very moment. A few days later Tina and Leigh's accounting instructor stopped me on the stairwell and asked me how I handle those two. She claimed their extreme drive to get everything correct made her physically sick. The bottom line—the two of them should have been at an Ivy League type school. They could have taught many of the classes in which they were enrolled. I'll always remember their herculean efforts, their competitive spirit, and willingness to laugh at a funny situation (particularly if the joke was on the professor.) They stayed in touch with me for a while and now have high-level positions in business.

Smaller institutions' faculty members wear a lot of hats. They teach, possibly coach, advise a club, serve on countless committees, and try to write some grants or publish articles or books. Unfortunately, this means going back to the office evenings and weekends. Some faculty members use the office as a refuge from a quarreling spouse or noisy kids. A very bright botanist friend used this time to play with his new toy—a scanning electron microscope—or at least he did until his wife caught him playing with it on Christmas Day. Even my wife admitted that I didn't go that far. I did slip away to the office most evenings—it seemed I needed to do so in order to be ready for the next day. I think my family suffered from my absences from the house. My wife occasionally came up to campus and, thankfully, dragged me home.

To make some extra dollars, several of the BH faculty drove to Ellsworth Air Force Base to teach extension classes in our respective disciplines. We generally transported ourselves in college-owned vans—two shifts a night Monday through Friday. The trip took a little over an hour one-way. One summer, a group of six males made the weekly trip. One Business Department faculty member was in a wheelchair. As luck would have it, one night the chair broke on arrival. Fortunately, the paraplegic fellow's good friend and Business Department colleague was also in the group. The friend, whom I'll call Richard, was a bit impatient that evening. Ari, the wheelchair bound professor, asked Richard to get him another chair. "They don't have any," Richard abruptly said.

"Then can you at least leave me one of the articles you have run off from *The Wall Street Journal?*" he begged.

"No," was the response. "I have just the right number for my class. Maybe," he continued, "the class could assemble out here in the parking lot and you could talk to them that way."

We left Ari in the car, but as soon as we were in the education building Richard called for and received a very modern wheelchair. He even said it was an emergency. I witnessed that night a combination of both irritation and affection between the two business faculty friends.

To help pass the time on the van, some of the Air Base faculty regulars would play the "Game." The game was played by one of the players thinking of a famous person and giving one hint about that person. Let's say the name was Babe Ruth. Players would guess the name of the personage but not directly, rather through a similar time frame, team, group, event, etc. So the group "leader" might say, "A famous baseball player known for his home-run hitting prowess." Someone might guess as follows: "Was it a person who wore pinstripes?" The person who had thought of the name originally might say, "No, it was not Lou Gehrig," and the game would continue with someone else guessing. If the player who was the leader couldn't think of a name to slough the clue off, he lost and was replaced by another guesser. However, whoever was "it" had to offer another clue. He might say for a clue "He is deceased." A guesser might counter with, "Was he a star of the 50s and 60s?" The leader could say, "No, it was not Roger Maris." The next clue might be, "He was not a star of the 50s and 60s." Eventually, someone might say, "Was he known as the Sultan of Swat?" Game over!

One night the van was carrying some of the "game" players as well as an elderly Eastern European professor who generally did not talk during the trip, Dr. G. He probably felt a bit out of place with the younger and more boisterous assistant profs, plus he had a decided accent. It soon became clear he wouldn't be playing the "game." As the game progressed, players got stuck on the person who had clues of a record-breaking athlete, not a native of the U.S., excels at a new Olympic event, is a female. After a period of dead silence, from the back of the van there came a voice with a thick

Slavic accent uttering, "Mar tina Navra ta lov a." The van exploded with, "Dammit, Dr. G., you weren't even supposed to be playing:" We laughed all the way to the air base.

The reason the College could count on faculty members to teach at the air base each term was that we were so poorly paid. The extension classes at the base paid extra and helped tide us over from paycheck to paycheck. Summer school was a similar situation; extra pay for extra duty. One summer early in my tenure there I thought I had the world by the tail. I was scheduled to teach the second half of an Integrated Science course for elementary teachers during the last half of the summer session. The first half session I was also scheduled to teach 5 one-credit science mini-courses. I also decided to teach a night biology class at the air base. Unexpectedly, there was an overflow to Part One of the Integrated Science class for teachers that I learned I could teach as well. I really was overloaded (16 credit hours) but I told my wife I could do it, and what a nice check we would have at the end of the summer.

Things started out OK but before long I was in over my head, time wise. With the attending paperwork, I was up until midnight correcting papers and preparing for the next day's classes. I rose about 6:00 a.m. I was mean, obstinate, and difficult to be around. Finally, the summer session came to an end and I told Mrs. D. to look forward to one big payday. When the last Friday of the summer rolled around, I was shocked to find that I had been paid for the air base course only. I was fit to be tied! I strode over to the administration building, brushed past the Provost's secretary, and walked into the central office. Unfortunately, he was with some influential parents who were planning upon sending their son or daughter to the school (until that day). I said, "What the hell is going on here? Can't this school get anything right? I worked my ass off all summer and for what? I got paid for 3/16 of what I should have been paid. Who is going to pay for all of our unpaid bills?"

The Provost, who until that day liked me, remained cool (probably the reason he was the Provost and I wasn't), asked me to calm down and excuse myself until the couple with whom he was meeting had completed their visit. Later that afternoon, with the help of the Provost and the Business Manager, I got my checks. I sheepishly thanked them both and high-tailed it out of there. Years later, after the Provost was speaking to me again, he told me that when he returned to the interrupted couple, they both looked shocked and said they had never seen anything like that before. At least I had made an impression on them. But I don't believe the son or daughter ever set foot on the campus.

Much of my summer teaching involved leading mini-course workshops for elementary teachers. These often centered on some specific area of biology such as botany, ecology, entomology, anatomy and physiology, genetics, the metric system, etc. Many of these lent themselves well to outdoor studies and field trips. A goal of these workshops was to utilize the school's surrounding environment in their teaching. On one such flower identification field trip we came upon the very rare spotted orchid. I pointed out the rare specimen to the group and talked about the diversity of plants and how each had its value to the ecosystem. Just then one of the teachers announced how Ginny (a local teaching friend) had picked the coral root. No, she denied. Someone (unnamed) had given it to her. Again, I stressed the value of each plant and how we can best serve nature by letting them be. I did add that it was unfortunate that the flower had been picked as it might well be the one and only such flower of that species that any of us would ever see. Just then as the path made a sharp turn leading into a broad green meadow, what should we see but a clump of at least 50 spotted orchids. Ginny and her unidentified flower-picking friend were not the only ones with egg on their faces that afternoon.

A requirement of a mini-course called "How to Know the Insects" was to collect 15 insects representing at least six orders. The night before the collections were due, our community was hit by a heavy hailstorm. One of the participants said she had to tend her garden during the storm and was one insect short, but that she had caught another "bug" that morning and could she please have a few extra minutes to get everything prepared. I said sure and forgot about her problem. I might add that many of the insect orders end with the suffix "ptera," which means wing. For example there is Diptera, Hymenoptera, Hemiptera, Coleoptera, etc. I had to laugh when I saw the teacher's "new" addition to her collection. It was labeled "Weedoptera" and, sure enough, she had created her own insect from pieces of weeds knocked off in the previous night's storm. The bogus insect actually looked better than some of the real insects in her and other students' collections. I wanted to write to an entomological journal and report that one of our teachers had found (created) a new insect order.

CHAPTER 4

Higher Education in the Equality State

After teaching several years at the small college in Dakota, I applied for and received a leave of absence to teach for a year at the University of Wyoming—a real research university! My duties were tri-fold: to teach a large biology section for the Zoology Department, to teach science methods classes for the College of Education, and to work in the Science and Mathematics Teaching Center offering classes that were inquiry based and often a hybrid science and education mix. I very much enjoyed my experience at U.W., particularly, my colleagues. They were bright, industrious, and very kind to me. It was not long before I was involved with them doing research, writing articles, and team teaching. Dr. Joe, Dr. Ron and I worked on a research project dealing with student science misconceptions. The professor I was replacing for the year (Dr. Alan) was the editor of a well-known science education journal. He was big into using magic as a teaching tool as well as right-brained, left-brained learning theory. Although he was on leave for a year, he came back to his office from time to time (I was using part of it). One day I asked him if he thought I was right or left-brained. He liked to ignore me so I was not surprised when he did not answer, but after about 20 minutes he offered this terse comment, "Neither," and left the office. I had asked for it. During my stay he treated me very well—as did everyone there.

In Dakota we used state-owned vans to ferry faculty to the air base and back; in Wyoming we flew to our extension destinations in small planes with a six or seven passenger capacity. On my night during spring (more like winter) semester six of us went to our various destinations on Thursdays. One fellow and a young female professor got off in Casper, plus we picked up a faculty member there. Another person got off in Riverton while my stop was Worland, up in the Big Horn Basin. The fellow who got on in Casper had the final destination—Powell. The pilot would eat dinner in Powell just as the class began and wait for that class to end. Then the stops coming back would be the opposite of those going out. We were told to be out on the tarmac and ready to go at a certain time (mine was 9:40 p.m.). There would be no waiting around for dawdling faculty members. The airports, other than Casper, were dinky places with one or two persons on duty. One Thursday morning in early March, Laramie was hit by a late winter blizzard. The temperature was below zero, winds were blowing well over 30 mph and visibility was poor. Faculty scheduled to fly that day were advised that we might not be going. However, about noon we were told that conditions were much better in other parts of the state, and if we could just get out of Laramie we would be OK.

Each week, faculty members took turns sitting in the co-pilot seat and would usually be invited to help read some of the plane's instruments. As luck would have it, that Thursday was my turn to sit in that seat. We took off in extremely soupy conditions. I could see nothing. Shortly after take-off the pilot told me that I would have to read the instrument panel closely and give him some readings. As we approached Casper, he said, "I don't know where we are, do you?"

I managed to gulp, "No."

Just then the clouds parted and I was amazed to see we were about two feet off the ground right smack in the middle of the runway. The pilot laughed and said, "I sure got you this time." He surely did. Of course, he knew all along exactly where we were, but he wanted to have a little fun with a smart-mouth college professor.

Later, I remember departing Casper in much better weather. In fact, the skies soon turned clear and off to the west I could make out the Grand Teton Mountains more than 200 miles away. Deplaning in Worland, I thought maybe I was coming down with a fever. I felt uncomfortably warm. I was wearing two winter coats, a lined hat, overshoes and gloves. The airport was adjacent to the city's golf course and people were playing golf. I couldn't believe it. The university representative assigned to pick me up shouted, "Hey Steve, are you dressed warm enough?"

"What is the temperature?" I asked. His response: "65."

Wyoming is a large state and the weather in the southeastern portion of the state (Laramie) can be very different from the weather in the much more moderate Big Horn Basin. Moreover, weather conditions can change rapidly in the mountainous west. Flying back, the pilot pointed out the lights of the various Wyoming towns that are few and far between. I learned a lot about Wyoming geography on those trips. I also learned not to fear flying in small planes—at least those flown by competent University pilots.

I remember a science education graduate student who had befriended one of my colleagues, Dr. B. The student was a minority member and a very nice guy. Unfortunately, his speech was difficult to understand. He had trouble with the letters L and R. One day he was giving an oral report about animals on the endangered species list. One such animal was the grey wolf, except he pronounced "grey wolves" as "gay oofs." Well, unfortunately for us, Dr. B. and I got the giggles whenever he would say "gay oofs" during the report. We both had to leave the room. Fortunately, we were able to time our adolescent laughter so that we were able to leave separately. The student wondered why we had both left the room during his report. We made up some story and assured him that he had done a good job, which he had.

I also remember this same young man had a slightly irritating habit of extending a conversation when it really should have been long over. He did this by saying, ". . . and one more thing." One sloppy spring day I encountered him in the library. I believe it was just a few days after Dr. B. and I had embarrassed ourselves over the "gay oofs" episode. Anyway, the student had a couple of questions for me. I was getting warm as I was wearing a heavy coat with a parka, gloves and overshoes. My wife had advised me not to wear the galoshes that day as most of the snow had melted, and that the overshoes squished when I walked and drew unwanted attention to myself. I wore them anyway, thinking I didn't want to get my dress shoes splattered. Besides, they were slippery and the overshoes gave me more traction. As I finished my conversation with the grad student (or so I thought), he said, ". . . and one more thing, why you wearing those noisy overshoes in the library?" Probably a "gotcha" for laughing at his "gay oofs" story a few days before.

Another cold winter day when I was again wearing my heavy coat with a parka, gloves, boots—the whole nine yards—I walked over to the building where my wife worked. She was a secretary in the Counseling Office. Students who were having academic problems went there as did some of the kids with different kinds of problems—including serious mental health issues. This particular day I went to the elevator and punched the button for the third floor. I should mention that with my parka up, I couldn't hear or see very well. When I arrived on the third floor, I could hear doors opening, but not the ones immediately in front of me. "What is the matter here?" I thought. I tried it once more. I again arrived at the third floor but the doors in front of me would not open, although I could hear doors opening. Finally, I started yelling and beating on the doors in front of me. "I want out of here!" I screamed. Then, I felt someone tapping my shoulder from behind. An elderly woman had tapped me and said, "The doors behind you open on these floors. You probably need to go to the Counseling Office immediately, don't you? Go right in there even if you don't have an appointment. I'm sure they can help you."

My wife was delirious when I told her what had happened. "Steve, only you could have done that," she laughed. She was right again, of course.

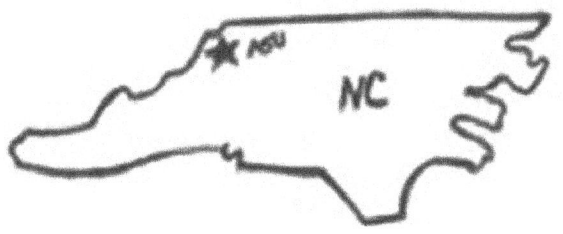

CHAPTER 5

◆

Quasi College Administration— Down South

Returning to Dakota was somewhat of a letdown. The folks at BH were nice but it felt like I had been there, done that—or as Yogi Berra might say, it was déjà-vu all over again. I missed the research university way of life. Some of the science misconception research that I had conducted with my Wyoming friends was beginning to be published, and I wanted in on the action. I did teach an extension science education course for U.W. at Gillette, Wyoming that fall and also maintained close contact with my colleagues at the Science and Mathematics Teaching Center. I really liked the Center concept as a way of helping both aspiring and bona fide teachers. I thought I would be interested in teaching at a center—either at U.W. or elsewhere.

I decided to look for another position. Our son was finishing high school that year so he would be gone in the fall, anyway. Dona was back at her job, day managing a popular restaurant, but she assured me she would be willing to move, at least to the right place. I was OK with my situation: nice kids, great boss, friendly colleagues, yet I felt something was missing. I applied for several positions that year looking for some of the things I mentioned previously. Another factor soon became paramount. Our son was accepted into Drake University in Iowa. His sister was already at Northwestern. So, with two kids attending expensive private universities it dawned on Dona and me that we needed bucks. Teaching in South Dakota was not going to supply them.

I interviewed for science education positions at four universities the spring and summer of 1985. The openings were in Connecticut, New York, California, and North Carolina. I was offered positions at the latter two. Neither of us had ever been to the Southeast, let alone lived there. The biggest attraction for Dona was that our best friends in Dakota had moved to southern Virginia to teach at universities there. Mrs. D. asked me to get out the atlas and see just how far it would be to our friends' house from this university to which I was applying. When I told her it looked like a little less than an inch on the map, she said, "Go for it!" Scale on a map, evidently, meant little to either of us.

I accepted the North Carolina position (Appalachian State University) in Boone. I was to be the Director of the Mathematics and Science Education Center and teach one class per semester in biology. My salary was almost twice what I had been able to make in Dakota. (The comparison is a bit unfair in that the S.D. position was for 9 months and the Carolina job was an administrative 12 month position.) I had a long history of bitching and moaning about how underpaid I had been over the years. My new salary made me giddy; sure, just peanuts to many in business and industry, but I felt well compensated. I never complained about my salary again. I remain an advocate for higher pay for public school teachers because most are hard working and very much underpaid and underappreciated. I, no longer, was either.

I moved to N.C. the end of August; Dona arrived a month later. She had stayed behind to finish her job at the restaurant, to close on the house and to sell our second car. We thought all went well until we received a call from our realtor advising us that our house sort of became unsold. We then had no cash for a down payment, so we lived in an apartment not much bigger than a walk-in closet. We had one bedroom with two single beds—not the best arrangement for entertaining family members or guests. Later that next spring when our S.D. house finally sold, we purchased a brand new home in the woods, yet it was right in town. I could walk to town or the university so we needed just one car. We lived in the house for 11 years. Maybe it just became too convenient, so we found another larger house five miles from town.

My final 25 years in education were spent at Appalachian State University, with the exception of one year when I taught at Brown University. My experience in the South was a positive one. I wore two hats: biology professor and Director of the Math and Science Education Center. In the latter, I arranged for or led workshops, institutes, and conferences in science and mathematics for teachers and/or kids.

Southern politeness was never more evident than the time a male student came in to see me after failing an exam. We visited for a minute before he asked what his grade would be for the semester. I had to tell him that it was an F. He got up to leave, smiled politely, and said, "Thank you very much, sir." I was flabbergasted. I really had more expected a protest, some pleading, an angry comment or even a punch in the mouth. Another time a young lady told me not to worry about the F that I had given her. "It was my fault, not yours," she said. "You are a good teacher," she continued, "I just don't get it."

One of my better students was a young lady from China who I will call Ana. Her English was not strong but she was very bright. She also had a good sense of humor. I called her my best Asian student (the only one I had in class that semester), and she called me her favorite biology teacher that she had that term. One day when we were studying the differences between DNA and RNA (DNA contains thymine [T], which is replaced in RNA by Uracil [U].) Ana mistakenly said there was thymine in RNA. I told her that although there is lots of tea in China, there is no T in RNA.

She said, "Dr. D., I do not find your attempts at making jokes particularly funny." However, when she returned to her seat she burst out laughing, and later in the period when she would look at me she would start to giggle. She exhibited intelligence with a great sense of humor—my kind of student.

One time when Halloween happened to fall on class day, I arrived early, dimmed the lights and hid behind the door. I was wearing a hideous-looking mask. When students entered the room I jumped out at them and gave them some candy. Most students got a chuckle out of it, but I scared another Asian female student so badly that she momentarily fell to her knees. She announced to the class, "I not like some of your American customs." Her classmates assured her that her other professors were not so crazy, and it probably wouldn't happen in her other more normal classes.

Sometimes I led workshops for elementary school kids. Center faculty often taught science concepts doing a stream study. One beautiful fall afternoon we were collecting aquatic specimens from a creek. One fourth grade guy found a crayfish and after the excitement of the initial discovery wore off, he started chasing a female classmate up the stream, creating all kinds of havoc. As I recall, most of the students were minority members and we had been having the best time. The female "victim" came up to me, screaming at the top of her voice to make the boy put the crayfish away. After considerable effort to calm the class, I began talking quietly about crayfish anatomy, males vs. females, etc. No sooner had I gotten the group settled down than the girl turned to the boy and said, "Do it again!" I just clamped my head in my hands and again gave thanks for letting me teach college students rather than fourth graders on a daily basis.

Appalachian State owns a facility on the Watauga River called Camp Broadstone. Its purpose is to provide a location for outdoor education and consists of a lodge (kitchen and dining hall plus basic meeting rooms), cabins for 75-100 people for overnight stays and an environment that allows for forest, field, and aquatic studies. The Camp served the Math and Science Education Center well in terms of a place to conduct science and math institutes for area teachers.

The state of North Carolina provides a small budget for each of the 11 Math and Science Centers located at university campuses. The Centers are staffed by a director, an assistant director, a secretary and some part-time personnel. The budgets were inadequate for what higher education administrators expected us to do. Therefore, to supplement the Centers' budgets, extramural funding is required. A major source of this extramural funding comes in the way of grants. A competitive funding source for the Centers (and all higher education institutions) were the federally financed Eisenhower Math and Science Education grants. Each grant ran for 12-15 months. They were usually rather small,

$25,000 to $35,000 annually, but were very helpful to the grant host institutions and enabled them to conduct in-depth teacher in-service for 15-20 teachers that they would otherwise be unable to do. Monies from these grants provided for teacher stipends, instructional materials, salary for faculty conducting the workshops, and travel expenses for teachers.

The Eisenhower program was in existence for 13 years, from 1987-2000, and served several thousand teachers in N.C. Each year, nearly a million dollars worth of grant money was made available through competitive grants. Competition was stiff, but the universities with Math and Science Centers had an advantage in that they were already geared up to serve teachers in those disciplines and had a strong track record of success in serving area teachers. In any given year, 20-30 proposals would be funded with Centers receiving the lion's share of the grants. I am proud to say that during my 19 years as the ASU Director, our Center received more than our fair share of grants—over 50 such proposals were funded and brought in well over a million dollars to our campus. I was lucky in that I had at my disposal some wonderful math and science faculty both at the university and public school level. I also was fortunate to have Camp Broadstone as a site to host many of our outdoor programs.

One year when we had several Eisenhower grants, we had many more teacher applicants than we had seats in our workshops. I was nervous about all of the applications and accidentally mixed up two teachers with the same last name. I sent one Ms. Johnson to a science workshop and the other Ms. Johnson to a math workshop—just the opposite of what they had applied for. I got Ms. Johnson #1 switched back to the correct workshop with no problem but Ms. Johnson #2 wasn't having any part of workshop swapping. I advised her that the workshop that she was mistakenly placed into was not as appropriate for her grade level, and it wasn't even the subject she wanted. "I know," she responded, "I like this one better. I have friends in there and the instructor is a little bit more interesting and a lot cuter than the other one." Regrettably, I let her stay in the wrong workshop.

Sometimes, the Centers found funding from sources other than the Eisenhower program. We had a three-year $180,000 proposal, a Women In Science program for female middle-grade teachers and their very best female students, funded by Burroughs-Wellcome pharmaceuticals. That program turned out to be one of the very best that our Center sponsored. We received strong support from two College of Education faculty, Elizabeth Long and Jeff Goodman. In fact, it was their idea for the proposal and they helped write the grant. Years earlier we had received funding for a two-year math and science grant for elementary teachers funded by Glaxo (now Glaxo-Smith-Kline).

Our Center had the opportunity to collaborate with other educational entities as well. We frequently conducted science workshops in connection with the traveling exhibits at the Catawba Science Center in Hickory. I became good friends with its very capable director, Mark Sinclair. I also knew his wife, Thea, an outstanding biology/chemistry teacher in the Hickory area. We worked with both Caldwell Community College and Lenoir-Rhyne College on the Women in Science program, and with the 19 school systems that made up our Center's service area.

The Center sometimes made use of private contractors, non-university folks who conducted teacher and student science and math activities for a profit. One of these was Diane Vaszily from Plantation, Florida. She ran an outdoor science program in the Everglades most of the year but came to the Carolina mountains for a week or two each fall. I sponsored her and set up a schedule of schools for her. She was so popular that she began bringing her assistant, Jeff Hugo, with her so that we could help meet the school demand for her services. Her programs were great—grade appropriate, hands-on in nature, and often held outdoors. Projects ran the gamut from identifying gems to making and launching rockets to studying animal skins. She was extremely dependable, punctual and professional in every way. One day (September 22,

1989) when she was scheduled at a school in a neighboring county at 8:00 a.m., my phone rang about 8:15. It was Diane and she was frantic. "I went to the school but it was dark and locked and it is very windy and it is raining very hard here. Do you think they forgot?"

"Diane," I countered, "have you not been listening to the radio?"

"No, I don't have time for that," she responded.

I told her that the National Weather Bureau had just announced that Hurricane Hugo was directly over us and that I wanted her to take shelter, then head back to Florida. In this case, being so very dependable could have produced serious consequences. She did go back to the hurricane-canceled school the next fall.

At the end of my first year at the Center we had some unspent salary money. I decided to bring in some nationally known math and science leaders and have a year-end extravaganza. I brought in two University of Wyoming hot-shots, Bob Kansky and Alan McCormack. Some of us ASU science and math educators performed as well. The extravaganza was a success and gave the Center a big boost. One of the final science events involved the careful manipulation of a raw egg in a relay-type race. At the very last minute, my egg broke and I truly had egg on my face, much to the delight of the teacher and student audience.

CHAPTER 6

◆

Special ASU Students

A couple of unusual occurrences on campus involved two male undergraduate biology students. The first instance took place during a final exam. It was a Saturday evening a few minutes into the exam. A short male student wearing a baseball cap and thick glasses demanded to take the exam. When I told him I didn't know him or even have him on my grade list, he became very agitated. I asked for his name, which he did give me, but I should have asked for his student photo ID. As he was bothering several of the students, I decided it would do no harm to let him take the test. He did, but when I corrected his exam he had, not surprisingly, missed most of the questions. I later found out that this little guy was using the name of another student from another class who had easily passed the course. When the small guy left he said to me, "I feel better about myself now." I never did figure it out.

The other event involved a confused and possible autistic kid I will call Freddy. Freddy was serious about biology. He would stay late (way late) after class to copy the notes from the board. He literally memorized those board notes and large sections of the textbook. Freddy would score well on tests that required recall and not so well on questions that needed some sort of application or analysis to solve a problem. One time he was furious with me when I couldn't tell him the page number in the text that was the source of a particular test item. Freddy was very literal in his thinking. I would say, "Freddy, you need to put two and two together to get the answer."

He would reply, "Well, this isn't a math class."

One cold day a female student and I were talking on campus when Freddy appeared while drinking some very hot coffee. He somehow managed to spill the coffee on the young lady's foot. As she screamed in pain, Freddy said, 'Darn, I spilled most of my coffee!"

Freddy wasn't into formalities, either. He referred to another biology professor as "Mizz Gordon" and to me as "Mister Dyche." One day Mizz Gordon took Freddy aside and pointed out that each of us had a doctorate so we should be called Dr. Gordon and Dr. Dyche. He nodded his head in agreement. The next week, when we saw him again, he greeted us with a "Hi Mizz Gordon" and "Hi Mister Dyche."

My teaching career has included working with many minority students. My self-assessment of that work is very positive. I grew up near an Indian reservation in southeastern Montana so I went to school with a number of Native Americans. Those folks from that area of the state prefer to be called Indians—or at least that is what they have told me. I had the privilege of playing basketball with arguably Montana's greatest player ever, Larry Pretty Weasel. In one game, Larry threw in 54 points but also led the team in assists. He stood 5'10" and weighed 155 lbs. He was extremely quick and very agile. My dad had coached at Hardin and also had great success in working with minority kids. One of my best friends was Native American. I also liked his two sisters. Of course in my short teaching experience at Busby, I worked with many Native Americans. Billings Senior had a few Hispanic kids, some

African-Americans and a smattering of Native Americans. At Black Hills State College, I had only a few minority students but many at both Appalachian and Brown.

My best-known minority student was Dex, an African-American defensive football player who enjoyed an all-pro career with the NFL Dallas Cowboys. Dex took my class as a freshman. He did not miss one class nor did he miss any of my weekly small student study groups. The only thing he missed was getting an A and he almost got that. He wasn't particularly interested or motivated by the instructor or the subject matter; he was just so darned competitive that he didn't want someone else to beat him on an exam. One time at his study group (it was a Sunday evening) Dex showed up with marks all over his face. I assumed them to be cleat marks from the Citadel game the day before. I did not see the game as it was away from home. Our team got stomped so I teased Dex about the marks on his face. He was very polite and answered me with, "Yes, sir, you are right, sir, I'll try harder next time, sir." He was very humble; he didn't bother to mention that he was named Freshman-of-the-Week for his game efforts, which included nine tackles, a quarterback sack, a hurry, and a fumble recovery. I didn't tease him after that, only a handshake for winning the Buck Buchannan National Defensive Player of the Year Award after both his junior and senior year.

When I called roll the first day of class, I noticed one female African-American student who, I recall, was named Roslyn Lake. She had neither a middle name nor initial by her name. I asked her about it and she said, "Just put down a G. for a middle initial." When I inquired why the G, she countered, "It stands for 'Great'. Get it professor Dyche? Great Lakes." Again, I have a bias for students with a quick sense of humor. It soon became obvious that Roslyn had more than a sense of humor. She usually had the top score on the class tests and went on to earn a graduate degree. She was one of my best students of all time.

A non-minority female classmate talked to me about Roslyn. "I don't like her," she said. "She always beats me on the tests and is a real grade grubber. She intimidates me."

A few days later while I was visiting with Roslyn, she said, "I don't care for that white girl who always beats me on the exams. She is a real grade grubber and she kind of intimidates me." Yup, we are talking about the same girl. Later, when they knew each other better, they became good friends. It didn't surprise me; they obviously thought alike.

Another African-American female student named Sandy was taking second semester freshman biology from me. She had a different professor first semester. After the second day of class I saw her working out in the student recreation area. She was on some apparatus or other, and I sat down next to her to try to let her know I was interested in knowing my students. I said, "Sandy, do you think you will pass my class?"

"Well yes," she said, somewhat indignantly.

"Well, who did you have for a professor last semester?" I queried. When she told me, I thought, "Oh, oh that guy never gives students a break." "And how did you do?" I finally worked up the courage to ask.

"Oh, I got an A; the only one in the class." "Sorry I asked," I thought. One other comment about Sandy; she told me that she was being cast as Othello in her class play. I said, "Wrong gender," and she replied, "But the right race." Again, I love students with a quick comeback and a sense of humor.

Still another African-American female student I will call Mary was beautiful and knew it. She was literally full of herself. She had won beauty contests, was one of a dozen co-eds who "ushered" at football games, etc. We clashed right off the bat. I expect all my students to work hard and try their best and she was having none of that. She missed class, gave me dirty looks and, I think, a bad evaluation. She made a D. We were definitely not on the same page. When I saw her on campus she sometimes spoke and sometimes not. In the early afternoon of the infamous 9/11 attacks, I was on campus going up a flight of outdoor stairs crowded with upset students and she was coming down the stairs which were divided by only a thin metal handrail. When she saw me her eyes lit up, and she reached across the handrail and gave me a huge hug. "Are you OK?" she asked. I assured her I was, even though folks in the three airplanes, the Pentagon and the Twin Towers were not. That gesture on her part started giving me that wet-eye problem again. The next home football game she came and sat with me for a while. I haven't seen her since graduation, but I did want her to know how much that kind hug meant to me on that terrible day.

Tina is a female African-American student who I recently taught. She is extremely petite. She was recently named the best athlete on campus by the student newspaper. Wait a minute, ASU is the three-time defending 1-AA college football national champion and several players have gone pro. Let me backtrack a bit. Biology 1101 introduced Tina to me. She was in a section of biology that made use of in-class study groups. Tina, unlike many of my students, came to see me during office hours in order to get some help. One day, she said, "Professor Dyche, you have stacks of non-alphabetized papers all over your office. Why don't I come in once or twice a week and organize them for you, and while I am here you can answer my biology questions." A true case of mutualism—we both benefited from the arrangement. She told me that both her parents were dead, her mom having died only a few weeks before college started. Her older brother called her daily to check on her. She told me she was at ASU on a track scholarship and that she participated in the long jump. I thought, "This little squirt—she couldn't be much." I did find that she was a good biology student. She scored high on exams and was always prepared. She also developed a fairly large circle of friends. One day, near the end of the semester, Tina told me that some very bright, hard-working white girls asked her to be in their study group next semester. She wanted to know if she should join them or not. I asked her why she wouldn't want to and she said, "I don't know if I am smart enough or even if they would want a minority student in their group."

I told her if that was the case, then they wouldn't have asked her in the first place. "Besides," I told her, "you are one of the best students in class and certainly one of the nicest. They would be lucky to have you." She did join the group and it was one of the finest that I had in years. Oh, yes, I forgot to mention, Tina won the indoor and outdoor Southern Conference long jump titles during her next three years of competition. Furthermore, her jumps were long enough to qualify her for the NCAA national finals. The school newspaper named her the best pound-for-pound athlete on the campus. Quite a feat considering that during her time at ASU, the football team won three consecutive national championships and defeated the University of Michigan in the Big House in Ann Arbor. Several of the players from that era went on to pro football careers in the NFL. The term "pound-for-pound" is important here. Tina only tips the scales at 95 pounds. She is currently applying for medical school. I hope that goes well for her. Even if it doesn't, Tina will wind up on her feet somewhere and spend her days helping others. In my opinion, there isn't a nicer person around.

A couple of African-American football players used to come to my office for help. I liked them both. One of the guys was a strong student and worked hard. Unfortunately, both of these young men got in trouble with the coach and were dismissed from the team. Sometimes I wonder what happened to those fellows. I wish them both well and hope they made amends.

My biology classes were divided (on a voluntary basis) into five-six person study groups. One particular group had five male students. Two were soccer players including an Asian-American, two were football players including an African-American, and the fifth member was a twirpy looking, 95-pound weakling type. I thought the combination of personalities and backgrounds wasn't a good mix and I feared for the twirp. Amazingly, the little guy was well liked (particularly by the football players). They always smiled at him, shook his hand vigorously and patted him on the back. He loved the attention from the campus jocks and flourished in the group. All members did rather well. The soccer players both got A's and made the all-conference second team. The football players easily earned their gentlemanly C's and the little guy made a B. A true team effort! Most of my all-male study groups did not function particularly well. This one was an exception.

Generally, the all-female study groups worked the best. For one thing, girls are more likely to join and regularly attend study groups than boys. Females, I think, like the socializing a bit more, and they tend to be more conscientious about their grades. Not always though. One winter's night several years back, a severe blizzard hit campus about dinnertime. An all-boys group was scheduled to meet at 8:00. I decided I would stay for it, primarily because conditions were very rough for walking the mile home, and my wife had the car. It appeared that no one was going to brave the elements to attend that night's study group. As I started to leave the building around 8:05, I saw two figures running towards the door. Both were so bundled up that I could not recognize them. Sure enough, it was two of the study group members: Two guys, one of which was a poor, somewhat lazy student (I thought); the other, a quiet, average-type biology student. I told the guys I was glad to see them and also surprised. They told me they were afraid to miss the study session and they knew they needed help. We worked together for over two hours that night and the students seemed to appreciate the help. On the cold walk home, I lucked out when a neighbor saw me and gave me a ride. Oh yes, the boys—the weaker student wound up with a hard earned C-, the other boy earned an A and a few years later graduated from law school at Chapel Hill.

One year, when I really had more study groups than I could handle, three young ladies who were having trouble with the class begged me to have a three-person study group. I suggested they join one of the already established groups. No, they felt insecure with others; besides, they all lived in the same dorm, so I could just come over a couple of times and help them out. I advised them that I would come one time to help. At the time, the spokesperson for the threesome had a low C, another girl had a D, and the third an F. When I met with them, I could see why they were having trouble. They had very few notes, which they had not reviewed, and they had not read their textbook. The questions they asked were very naïve and often pointless. After an hour-long lesson on note taking, study habits, review time, etc., I was convinced the girls wanted to do better. So I relented and came back for a second session, and a third and a fourth. By semester's end, the young lady with a low C was now in high C territory, the D student had shot up to a B (with an A on the final), and the young lady with an F had climbed to a low C. The three sweeties thanked me profusely and I marked the group experience for them as a success. The payoff, however, came the next fall when the young woman who had made the B in the course saw me on campus and ran up to me to tell me that she was enrolled in a kinesiology class. That morning the professor had asked the class about the Krebs Cycle. She said, "Guess what, Dr. Dyche? I was the only student who knew! You pounded it into my head last year and it stuck."

Speaking of the Krebs Cycle (a series of reactions carried on in the cell's mitochondria that are a part of aerobic respiration), a good friend and colleague from the College of Education and I were enjoying a pizza at a campus watering hole one day. He wondered if I thought it was valuable to teach about Krebs and all of the memorization of chemical names and reactions that it entailed. I agreed; I had my doubts, and we both thought that the forest was often lost in the trees. I noticed the cashier was a student I had in freshman biology a couple of years earlier. Although she had done well in the class, she was not a biology major and had not taken subsequent science classes. Jeff, my friend, said, "When we cash out, let's ask her what she remembers, if anything, about the Krebs Cycle."

I said, "OK, but this could be embarrassing to both her and me." When asked, she burst into a smile and said the Krebs Cycle was part of aerobic respiration in which high energy compounds were made in preparation for the formation of ATP. Jeff and I were shocked. I didn't think she knew that much about the topic when she was actually taking the class! I said in a voice loud enough to be heard by all that she was just a typical, average student of mine (she knew I was kidding). When reminded of that incident a couple of years later, she admitted she wasn't sure about the Krebs Cycle that day, but it just popped into her mind. She added that had we asked on another day she probably wouldn't have remembered. I tell the story not to strengthen the cause for teaching the Krebs Cycle (I actually agree with Jeff), but to point out the ironies of teaching and working with some wonderful students.

Just a couple of years back, I had another particularly positive experience with a study group. As I remember, the group met fairly late in the evening in the campus library. There were only five people in the group, two males and three females. They met every Monday night whether I was coming or not and often continued their session until close to midnight. If I wasn't there, they would have questions for me the next morning in class. They were probably the most self-motivated group that I ever had. Besides being strong students, they were all super-nice kids. I thought highly of all of them. The real kicker was the time when the campus was on lockdown due to a report of a threatening gunman, later reported to be totally fictitious, and the group called me at home and wondered why I wasn't in the library at their session. Talk about focused on biology!

MSEC

CHAPTER 7

◆

The Center

During my 19-year tenure as Director of the Mathematics and Science Education Center, I was served by three different secretaries: Jan, Pam, and Judy. All were good and had different strengths that they brought to the job. Judy served the longest and was the most recent. On her good days she had a great sense of humor and liked to tell stories about herself. She also suffered from numerous ailments. Occasionally, she took sick leave. One day when she was out, I was busy packing up a load of boxes stuffed with science equipment that I was going to use at a teacher workshop "off the mountain" early the next morning. Judy was home that day and didn't observe my tedious packing. My plan was to have everything ready so that I could get the state car, load it and be off bright and early the next morning. I left the mountain of packed boxes in the resource room that night, all ready to go for the next day. When I got to my office the next morning, I was stunned to find all of the many boxes unpacked with the goodies all placed back on their respective shelves. Judy had come in that evening and, thinking I had come back from a workshop, was going to spare me the time and trouble of putting all of that science stuff back. We normally communicated well, but obviously not that time except for the choice words I used that next morning.

Another time, Judy was complaining of a bad back and had gone to the doctor's to see about it. He had prescribed some exercises, one of which required another person to gently place a foot in the small of her back. So, she drafted me to be the foot placer. This particular day, students were on spring or fall break and nobody seemed to be around. Judy said she was supposed to do her exercises and wanted to know if it was OK to do them on her office floor, and could I help with the foot-in-the-back thing. I saw no problem with it. Of course, at the critical time, with my foot planted firmly in Judy's back, in walked a very critical, no-nonsense elementary teacher who had the day off and came up to the Center to check out some materials. She didn't say anything but gave us looks as if we were a couple of wackos. The most unbelievable part of the story comes next. Several weeks later, I hurt my back trying to lift some heavy boxes. Judy suggested that I try her exercises since they had worked for her. This time, I was on my office floor and Judy had her foot in my back, and who should walk in? You guessed it—the same elementary teacher who was now returning her checked-out materials. She uttered not a word but never did return to the Center. Judy and I wondered if the mental health folks on campus might want to visit us to see if we were really all right. We often wondered what the chances were of the same person witnessing each of us, several weeks apart, with our foot in the other's back? A good problem for our statistics faculty, I guess.

Another time, when Pam was the Center secretary, she had helped me get material together as part of the preparatory work for submitting seven math and science education grant proposals. Because our budgets were small, the availability of extramural funding was eagerly sought by all of the N.C. Math and Science Centers. The proposals took several weeks to prepare and the competition was keen (see Chapter 5). The funding of any one of the grants meant an extra $35,000 for Center use. The downside of getting proposals funded is that you have to carry out what you promised you would do. This amounted to a heck of a lot of work—much of it done by the office secretary. It often involved a good deal of time spent after working hours. The day that we were to hear about the fate of the grant proposals finally arrived. Pam was out to lunch (she often said I was the one "out to lunch") when the call came. I couldn't believe the news—six of the proposals were funded and the seventh was top alternate and probably would be funded, too. I let out a yelp just as Pam came in the door. "What is it?" she cried. "Are you OK?"

I told her we had the most unbelievable good news, great news. "Well, what is it?" she asked.

I told her that all seven of the grants were being funded. Without batting an eye she inquired, "Well, what is the *good* news?" I guess it all depends on one's perspective.

One of our Center's most successful programs came from a grant funded by the pharmaceutical giant, Burroughs-Wellcome. The program, Women in Science, was geared for 24 female middle-school science teachers and 48 middle-school girls. The program ran for three years and included several all-day Saturdays during the academic year and three weeks of all-day summer study. The capstone of the grant was a two-week work experience in a science-based business. Teachers received stipends and several hundreds of dollars of science apparatus. Each Saturday session was devoted to physics/astronomy, chemistry, geology, biology, or computer science. Faculty members, generally women, from ASU science departments led the sessions.

The grant was written by Dr. Elizabeth "Lib" Long, and Jeffrey Goodman of the College of Education, and myself. In my opinion, this program had a broader impact on teachers and kids in our area than any other mathematics or science project that we had undertaken. We had two cadres of teachers and female students, but we wanted to have some activities where both groups could be together and meet one another. In addition to an all-day hands-on science session, it was decided to have a dinner for both groups as well as the students' parents. To highlight the evening, we would invite a woman scientist to speak to us. Several names were suggested, but the name that came up most often was Joanne Burkholder, the well-known Pfisteria researcher from North Carolina State University. I volunteered to try to contact Dr. Burkholder but thought there was no way she would come. Much to my surprise, she immediately said yes. She did come and speak with us on an evening not to be forgotten. There was much interest in her talk, as evidenced by teacher drawings left on the paper tablecloths to communicate some of Joanne's thoughts to their students. After the talk was given, several rounds of kudos received, and awards presented, I was greeted by a kiss on the cheek from Joanne. I didn't wash my face for several days—until my wife finally made me do it.

The next fall, Dr. Burkholder returned to the ASU campus to deliver the annual Convocation Address. The book, *The Waters Turned To Blood*, which chronicled her Pfisteria research that later left her embattled with the North Carolina governor and her career up in the air, was required reading for ASU's incoming freshmen. I was more than pleased that when I was about to be introduced to her, Joanne's eyes lit up with recognition and she said, "I already know this guy." That definitely was the height of my rubbing-shoulders-with- famous-scientists days. (I also had the privilege of meeting James Watson, Jim Fowler, Harold Urey, Bill Nye the Science Guy and Ralph Bunche, although the latter was not a scientist.) Joanne was much prettier than any of those "greats" listed above.

One time in the category of "It's funny now but wasn't then," the Center had a brush with the law. A mycologist from the ASU Biology Department and I were driving to a town 50 miles distant to conduct a mushroom workshop at the Catawba Science Center. Along the way, we spotted two State Trooper cars parked along the road and the two troopers seemed to be visiting. "What a waste of taxpayer money. They are having coffee at our expense," I said. My mycologist buddy agreed. About a half-mile down the road an older model large car passed us at a high rate of speed. Just then, we saw the flashing blue lights and heard the sirens of the two patrol cars. We came to a stoplight and the trooper cars slammed to a vee-stop right in front of the older car that had just passed us. The troopers jumped out with guns drawn and pointed. One of them held a huge, loud, barking guard dog on a leash.

Just then, a Sheriff's car with two men inside approached on a side road to the left. One of these gentlemen held a high-powered rifle that seemed to be pointed right at us. Just in front of us, the patrolmen threw three guys out of the car but let the driver, a woman, stay in the vehicle. The now unleashed dog started to sniff the inside of the car. My friend, John, the mycologist (I would have preferred John the Baptist right then) said, "Steve, if they shoot, I hope they won't shoot high 'cause we are right in the line of their fire." I told John to give me my driving glasses. When he asked me why, I told him that if we were arrested or shot I wanted to look like I was observing the law. After about 45-50 minutes had passed, all of the car's passengers, including the woman, were handcuffed and taken away in police cars. We were allowed to go on our way. We never heard more about the incident. We concluded that it was probably a drug bust—one that was almost foiled by two unwitting college professors.

Unbeknown to us, our non-arrival at the Catawba Science Center had caused quite a stir. We Center folks had a reputation of always being on time, if not early, to workshops. When our time of arrival came and passed, the CTC folks called Judy back at our ASU office (this was prior to cell phone technology). No, she replied, we had left in plenty of time to get to Hickory. Folks at both ends got nervous. After being nearly an hour late, we showed up. We were greeted very warmly; in fact, the CSC folks carried in all of our heavy boxes for us so we could get set up for the workshop. "Car trouble?" we were asked.

"No," we replied. "A drug bust."

"Come on, big guy," said CSC Director, Mark Sinclair, "you can come up with a better story than that. Admit it, you stopped for a couple of cool ones."

Funny, how truth is stranger than fiction.

MSEN

CHAPTER 8

♦

The Math and Science Education Network

The Math and Science Education Center that I directed was part of a larger organization called the Mathematics and Science Education Network (MSEN), which was headquartered in Chapel Hill. Centers were strategically placed at state universities around North Carolina so that no teacher would be more than 75 miles from a Center. During my tenure with MSEN, I served under four Network Directors, Vinetta J., Susan F., Gerry M., and Verna H., all of whom held earned doctorates in math, science, mathematics education, or science education. In my opinion, all performed their duties to the best of their abilities and helped move the Network forward. Nothing in particular comes to mind about any of them being involved with overly humorous situations but they did supervise the Network when some funny occurrences took place.

Vinetta J. had the habit of calling me on the phone about two minutes before 5:00 P.M. I initially thought it was to check to see if

I was in my office. More accurately, it was just her way of winding down after a very busy day. When I shared Dr. J.'s habit with my wife, she, too, started calling me about 5:00. One day she disguised her voice and announced herself as Vinetta. I must have visited with her for two or three minutes before I realized that Mrs. D. was playing a trick on me.

Another time, early in my tenure, after a long Director's meeting led by Dr. J., I got up to leave but could not find my coat. I saw my friend, Floyd M., the Director at East Carolina University, and thought he was wearing my coat. He insisted it was his and said it was a London Fog brand. "So is mine," I retorted, "and mine has a rip in the pocket just like this one."

I literally tried to take his coat off him but was interrupted by my assistant, Terry Carroll, who announced to the world, "I found Steve's coat in the men's room." After that, I wish he would have left it there. Fortunately, Dr. M., among his many good qualities, did not hold a grudge. I often wondered what he thought about the newbie Director at ASU after that embarrassing episode.

Ironically, that same coat almost was lost on two other Network occasions. During the 1992-93 academic year, I took a leave of absence from ASU to teach at Brown University. That October, I flew back for our semi-annual Advisory Board meeting. Susan F. was there, too, and after the meeting offered to drive me back to the airport. We were so busily engaged in MSEN business that I forgot the coat and left it in her car. She was kind enough to mail it to me at her expense, of course.

A few years later, the coat was left at a meeting in Burlington and, fortunately, found and recognized (it had a fame of its own by now) by my friend from the State Department of Education, Brenda E. She, too, mailed me the coat at her time and dollar expense. I think that by this time it would have been cheaper for someone just to buy me a new coat. Actually, my wife did purchase me a new trench coat, but I wouldn't wear it—too many memories tied to the old model.

The era of MSEN that I enjoyed the most was the regime of Dr. Gerry M. 1995-2000. It might have been due to Gerry's gender and his academics (science education) that I found a greater kinship with him, or maybe it was his relaxed personality. Anyway, we co-edited a couple of botany books and had great fun with the project. He did most of the background work and I took most of the glory. One year, due to Gerry's leadership in the National American Biology Teachers Association, we were able to host the national meeting of that group in our own backyard, Charlotte. I enjoyed helping Gerry with this program. Some of the other Center Directors did not appreciate Dr. M.'s laid-back leadership style, but I certainly did. Unfortunately, MSEN lost some of its stature in the state during that time. Maybe this was because we were seen as nice guys and nice guys make easy targets. This was also a time of great emphasis on End of Year Tests forced upon the state's public schools. Since science was not regularly a part of these tests, it often did not get taught at the elementary or middle school levels as much as it should. As a consequence, science workshop requests for teachers came less often to the MSEN Centers. Interestingly, Eisenhower grants awarded to the ASU Center increased dramatically at this time.

One semi-humorous incident that I recall from the Gerry M. years was at one of the first Network meetings over which he presided. It was in Chapel Hill and I drove in just as Gerry was arriving. He jumped out of his car and greeted me with a warm handshake. Now, I am not saying Gerry was nervous about the impending meeting but I noted that his car was still running. I asked him if his car was one of those new models whose engine cuts off after the ignition is disengaged. No, he said, it wasn't. I suggested that he turn his vehicle off. A strange look came over his face and he replied, "I can't, the keys are still in the ignition!" He thought to call AAA, who advised him to go to his meeting, and they would attend to his locked car. As I recall, when we came out of the meeting, Dr. M. seemed pleased that his car engine was no longer running. Unfortunately, when we approached the car he found that it was still locked and the keys were in the ignition. Bottom line—the car had run out of gas and AAA could not locate the vehicle. Dr. M. took it in stride.

An incident with Dr. Verna H. that at the time was not at all funny, but one that we could laugh about later, involved a pre-Labor

Day weekend message from her to me. Her Network office had been instructed on Friday afternoon to obtain an enormous amount of data from each MSEN Center in order to justify their existence. I received the news just before 5:00 P.M. that Friday, and the material was to be in Verna's hands the following Tuesday. My wife and I had planned a long weekend with our daughter, son-in-law and our two grandchildren. I saw red and immediately e-mailed Dr. H., advising her that I had previous commitments and was not going to follow the directive. The message was sprinkled with a few choice expletives. A return message from Dr. H. advised me that such talk was not appropriate or appreciated.

As so often happens with me, going back to my days as an athlete, I talked a much better game than I played. I wound up spending the weekend at the office, gleaning information for MSEN and filing a rather thorough report. Verna appreciated my effort, if not my words, as it got her superiors off her back, although I'm sure not a single word of the voluminous report was ever read. Of course, I apologized for the inappropriate words and tone of my earlier message. At the next Director's meeting Verna greeted me with a bear hug that literally squeezed all of the residual air out of my lungs. We got along great after that. I learned to appreciate that she was trying to save the Network. After that, whenever she said she had some homework for the Directors, I would always ask if she was going to assign it for Labor Day weekend and, thankfully, she always laughed.

Several of my Center Director peers at the other state universities were good for a few laughs from time to time as well. All were good leaders but each had his/her own style that sometimes surprised the rest of us. Dick W. at UNC Wilmington had a background in chemistry and administration and knew how to get things done. Dick was also very clever with technology tools and was the unofficial Network leader in the use of technology in science education. At one Director's meeting he showed up with a female assistant director to help him demonstrate the technology to us. I was always a bit intimidated by machinery of any kind and was easily wowed by the Wilmington pair. The next day, as they were preparing to return home, I noticed the assistant had put a suitcase by the front door of the hotel. I thought I might impress her with my chivalry and get some good technology tips by taking her bag out to their state car. As I was walking away I heard Dick say, "That was very nice of Steve to carry my suitcase out to the car for me." Obviously, I didn't earn any brownie points with the assistant nor did I get any tips, technology or otherwise, from either of the UNC-W folks. At least I tried; besides, I said I wasn't any good with technology. Evidently, the same was true for my abilities in identifying luggage.

Another good egg was Dr. Katherine H. at East Carolina University. Katherine was a well-known mathematics educator in the state. She was from Alabama and was "old school" about running a no-nonsense program. When I met her, she was Floyd M.'s (of my overexposed trench coat fame) assistant director. Katherine did not say much but when she did, everyone listened. She had a reputation for thinking things through and then when speaking, hitting the nail directly on the head. She would occasionally let her hair down with some of the rest of the Center Directors by having a drink or two after the meetings. One time during one of the state's financial belt-tightening times, she and Floyd announced that they were sharing a room at the hotel. It was purely a money-saving move but we all got a kick out of the announcement. Unfortunately, Katherine was stricken with cancer a few years later and ultimately died from the disease. I liked her a lot. Katherine's successor at ECU was Dr. Karen D. She modeled herself after Katherine and was also from Alabama. I always thought that the Center at East was fortunate to have three consecutive leaders of the quality of Floyd, Katherine, and Karen.

Another good Center Director was Dr. Jo W. at UNC Charlotte. Jo was friendly, lively, and pretty. Unfortunately, she later met the same fate as Katherine H. Once, Jo was hosting a big science extravaganza for state science teachers. Both Math and Science Network Directors and State Department of Education folks were assisting. On the Sunday evening prior to the event, it was discovered that we needed several large plastic bowls in which to place crushed ice. Jo gave Bill T., from the Department of Public Instruction, and me the task of purchasing some bowls from some nearby store—Big Lots, K-Mart, Lowe's, somewhere. Bill was a pretty smart guy so I thought the task would be easily accomplished. However, after marching up and down every aisle of a three-acre superstore we could not locate the plastic bowls. Finally, desperation overcame pride and we asked one of the store employees where the large plastic bowls for placing crushed ice were located. He calmly told us to turn around and look up. Here we saw a huge sign with the words "Large Plastic Bowls." The employee looked at us as if we could not read. So my parting comment was, "Yes, but it doesn't say if we can put crushed ice in them or not." I'm glad neither of us knew anyone in the store.

Vallie G. was the Center Director at UNC Greensboro; her background was chemistry and she had co-authored a number of science books for elementary school kids. Her reputation went back further than that. She was involved in the famous Woolworth's lunch counter sit-in of the 1960s in Greensboro. She was plenty brave to do that. Vallie was also a nice person and would do anything for anyone. She had a problem, though, of being chronically late. No doubt she had a busy agenda but nevertheless she was always late—sometimes several hours late. One time, we had a Director's meeting in Greensboro, and Ralph D. from Western Carolina University and I both arrived at 1:05—five minutes late. Much to our surprise, who was already present and seated? None other than Vallie. Ralph leaned over to me and whispered, "Partner, we must be a full day late in order for Vallie to beat us here." Neither of us could believe that the two of us, with records of being punctual could arrive after Vallie. The other Directors gave us both a good roasting that meeting.

Not long after moving to North Carolina, I took up jogging during my noon hour. I began with a small group of other paunchy, middle-aged men and women. We would run a half-mile, then walk a while, run another 880 yards, walk again and run one more-half mile. Within a few weeks most of us were able to go three miles without stopping—albeit at a very slow pace. I finally got my time down to about a 7:30 mile. I felt better about myself, lost between 15 and 20 pounds, felt healthier, and made some great friends (misery loves company). I even tried a few 5K races and one time placed third in my age category. I reluctantly mention that one guy who could always beat me was out of town and another got sick near the end of the race and couldn't continue. My wife entered the races as a walker and won some medals. Our daughter and son also participated in a few of the runs. We drove out of town for a couple of races.

Many years later while jogging, I discovered that there was something not right about my health. One day, I seemed out of breath after not running particularly far and I was going way too fast. I couldn't seem to slow down unless I flat-out stopped. When I tried to slow to a walk, I continued to go at a pace much faster than normal. Another day, I literally ran over a female student; I just couldn't control my pace. A few weeks later at a football game my right hand started to tremble, and it has continued to do so off and on for the last four years. When I get nervous, the condition becomes more pronounced. At the urging of my daughter, son, and a nurse friend at church, I went to my doctor to get things checked out. He had me take a few steps then immediately referred me to a neurologist. The diagnosis: Parkinson's Disease—right up there with Michael J, Fox, Mohammed Ali and a million others more including my friend Bernie in Montana. In a way it was sort of good news—the mystery was solved, plus I had half expected something worse.

So, I still jog but at a much slower pace and for a much shorter distance. I no longer run long enough to get a runner's high, but it breaks up my day and I at least think I am doing my body some good; besides, the tremors stop while I am running. I now also box twice weekly. The humor in all of this: Students who were spectators at the 5K races I used to enter would have looks of great surprise (and amusement?) when they saw me in a race, probably thinking, "If this fat old fogey can run a 5K, it couldn't be too hard."

One other witticism about my health condition, and perhaps why my wife didn't pick up on it sooner: When Dona was asked by the neurologist if she noticed anything different about me, she replied, "Well no, he has always been such a bumbler, I didn't notice anything unusual at all." That is funny because it is so true—I have been a fumbler all my life. It is a small miracle that I could play ball even at the mediocre level at which I played.

CHAPTER 9

Science Education at Brown University

After spring semester of 1992, I accepted a one-year position at Brown University. I was to teach, recruit, and counsel graduate students into Brown's Master's of Art in Teaching (MAT) program in Biology. I knew my predecessor, Grace T., and I believe she spoke favorably on my behalf for the position. I was given a leave of absence from ASU for one year, July 1-June 30.

What was humorous about my year at this very fine, elite Ivy League school was that I was there at all. I had applied for a position at Brown a couple of years earlier but was not selected. I was told at the time that my major strength was my good sense of humor. Most of the students with whom I worked had higher IQ's than my body weight. Most were very nice and patient as were the professors. I even had one senior tell me the best thing about his senior year was his chats with me. No, he wasn't deranged, just different. He was working on a special project designing a science room for kids in a Baltimore science museum. I believe I gave him a couple of ideas he could use.

One neat assignment that I had at Brown was to co-teach a class entitled Women in Science. The other instructor and the student adviser were also males. The class was all female. To say that we males taught the class would be a misnomer. We sort of guided the discussion. The students actually taught the class. They were all very bright and extremely hard working. A major concern of the Women in Science class was the low number of females enrolled in the hard sciences at Brown. Many of the young women enrolled in those classes opted out after only a semester or two. Sometimes, the women dropped out due to unkind remarks made by male classmates or even the professors themselves. Through a campus-wide survey of science students, it was found that one thing that seemed to help the female students stick with the science classes was the formation of small study groups, preferably all female or at least the majority needed to be female.

These Women in Science students at Brown heard there was a similar class at Holy Cross University. They thought they might have a joint meeting to compare findings, share experiences, etc. They decided to set up a weekend retreat in April with their Holy Cross counterparts. One of the young ladies was nominated to make the invite. I should point out that 7 of the 12 class members were Jewish, including one Asian student. At the next class meeting, bad news was received by the class. No, the Holy Cross class could not meet that weekend; it was Good Friday. The Brown students were mystified. Why couldn't they meet on Good Friday? That was two days before Easter. I didn't see humor in this incident, but the point was driven home to me that the Jewish students were as ignorant of some Christian observances as the Christian students were of Jewish holy days.

With respect to the study groups, I was so impressed with them that I used them in my freshman biology classes back at ASU the next fall and continued to use them for the rest of my teaching career. I am convinced they improve student learning for all students, not just females. The study group interactions did make for some humorous incidents.

I had two counterparts at Brown. I directed the MAT program in biology, Lee directed a similar program for English, and David did the same for social studies. All three of us 50+—aged guys reported to a woman named Nona. We all got along fine except David and Nona. In fact, he succeeded in getting her fired and I really don't know why. Anyway, we three fellows met weekly to compare notes and plan strategy for our classes and recruitment programs.

We usually got along as Lee and I were easygoing. Lee had polio in high school and got around on crutches. He was very considerate to all. David and I also got along quite well. He joined my wife and me for some social occasions and had us over for Thanksgiving dinner. Lee and David were both Brown alums, and they liked to tell me that it was much easier to get a teaching job at Brown than it was to be admitted as an undergraduate—knowing full well that I had not attended Brown. Incidentally, I believe they were correct.

I always felt a little overwhelmed and overmatched when I was on campus, although I do believe I did a good job. Lee told me once that the students really enjoyed the down-home personality that I employed around them. If he and they only knew it was the only personality that I had, they may have been disappointed. Both students and faculty were very nice to me there and always treated me respectfully.

On the plus side, teaching at Brown had its advantages—I'll call it the prestige factor. One time I was asked by a middle school science teacher friend to testify against an anti-vivisection bill that was being introduced in the Rhode Island State Senate. I was happy to do it because I have strong feelings about the matter. As I began my testimony at the State House, I was asked by one of the bill sponsors by what authority did I speak, and where did I teach, anyway? As soon as I said I was on the faculty at Brown, the hearing room became completely quiet. I immediately sensed there would be no more future questions about my credibility. Bottom line—the bill, as we had hoped, was voted down. Had I said I taught at any one of the other institutions where I have been employed, I fear that my testimony would have been less respected, and the vote on the anti-vivisection bill might have been quite different. So, I guess in this case, it wasn't who you are but where you are.

Another area where the prestige factor may have kicked in was grant proposals. Yes, I had some luck at my two previous schools in grant writing, but I felt that the two proposals that I drafted at Brown were enhanced by the fact that they were written at and supported by the university. One was an Eisenhower Math and Science proposal utilizing the ongoing program at Brown Summer High School. The other was a proposal to the U.S. Department of Energy. This one involved a partner organization in science. Fortunately, I had made friends with the folks at Save the Bay. They wanted to partner in a hands-on science project at which students and teachers were taught to monitor Narragansett Bay. The proposal included short boat trips out into the bay to sample the water both chemically and through invertebrate population studies. I honestly believe that without the name of this fine Ivy League university, neither proposal would have been funded. Again, it seems that it matters not as much who you are as where you are.

My predecessor as Director of the MAT program at Brown was Grace T., a seasoned biology teacher from the greater Boston area. The summer I worked with her was an Olympic year, and she kept close tabs on the USA basketball team. The reason: one of its star players, Patrick Ewing of Georgetown University and New York Knicks fame, had been a student of Grace's several years before. Grace had a rather high, squeaky voice but she was a master teacher. We didn't agree about everything but, in general, our teaching philosophies were similar. I learned many things about teaching from Grace. I still employ many of them to this day. She paved the way for me that next year, especially in setting up good relationships with the area public schools. Dropping her name to school principals made it easy to get the Brown MAT candidates placed in student teaching positions.

A real bigwig in the Education Department at Brown was Ted Sizer. Dr. Sizer was the former Dean of the College of Education at Harvard, former Headmaster at Andover, and had held many other prestigious education positions. He is best known for his book *Horace's Compromise,* from which the term "less is more" in educational offerings is derived. Much of Dr. Sizer's philosophy is incorporated into Brown's MAT programs. He was quoted, almost weekly, by *The New York Times,* The *Boston Globe,* or the *Christian Science Monitor.* I am not saying I was bosom buddies with the man, but we had breakfast together a couple of times and "talked things over." I'll always wonder what the heck was going through his mind at those times.

Tuesday evenings were usually fun as my wife and I helped Biology Professor Dr. Peter H. with a dormitory food fest. Professor H. was a live-in faculty adviser for a dorm. Tuesday evenings we would have an informal session featuring snacks for the residents, plus some sort of entertainment such as campus singing, dancing groups, a short skit or brief talk, or maybe a sing-along. Dona and I were privileged to see the daughter of James Taylor and Carly Simon, the son of Morley Safer, and dozens of very nice kids. A few years earlier we might have met John F. Kennedy, Jr. or Amy Carter.

CHAPTER 10

Some Special Colleagues

In addition to teaching so many talented and good-humored students, the opportunity to work alongside some outstanding colleagues is a career highlight. One such colleague is my late friend, Dr. Edgar Greene. I met Ed when I flew to ASU to interview for the Center Director position. He was a good guy and we had similar backgrounds. Both of us had taught high school biology, had terminal degrees in science education, and were the same age. Additionally, he was a very good instructor and enjoyed working with teachers. He was also a good person to know as his wife, Dr. Joyce Lawrence, was the Dean of the Graduate School. It was good for the Center to have support in high places.

One of my first workshop experiences with Ed was one that for some reason had attracted several older, prim and proper female middle school science teachers. I should mention that Ed was not very reverent and he peppered his presentations with some oaths. "Damn it, Steve," he would frequently say when irritated with me. At this particular meeting we were trying to tie mathematics and statistics into biology teaching. A question came up about how you could do this with a topic like mitosis. Ed suggested counting the number of cells undergoing each stage of mitosis on a microscope slide and then using the Chi Square method of testing statistical significance. Although it sounds complicated, it is fairly straightforward and can be done by bright middle school students. I was so excited about Ed's idea that I somewhat rudely blurted out, "Yeah, we used to do that years ago when I taught in Montana." Ed thought that I was ridiculing his idea as being old hat, but I was really excited about his answer. Ed's off-the-top-of-his-head response was, "Steve Dyche, you can go to hell." Although neither of us thought anything about it, there were some loud gasps and wide-open mouths from some of the more prim members of the group. One lady asked me after the workshop if Ed and I actually got along. I assured her that we were the best of friends. Years later when I was presenting Ed with the ASU Alumni Award, a few days before his death, he said, "Steven, thank goodness you didn't tell everybody about the time I told you to go to hell." I retorted, "If I had thought of it, I would have told the entire story."

Another time, Ed and I, along with a geology professor, John Callahan, led a middle school outdoor science workshop at Camp Broadstone. Early in the day we had explored the Watauga River looking for aquatic invertebrates, crayfish, stoneflies, mayflies, freshwater shrimp, snails, etc. The teachers liked the activity and were impressed by the variety of life we had found. That afternoon, Dr. C. also took the teachers to the river. He talked about the chemical makeup of rocks and how being in a river bottom for thousands of years could shape the rocks. John pulled a large, fairly flat rock from the stream and began talking about its geologic properties. Soon there were gasps and much finger pointing by the audience. A huge stonefly (much larger than anything we had seen that morning) was crawling across the surface of the rock. Dr. C. brushed it away without comment as if he had not even seen it and continued with his geology lecture. I tell this story because for the first time in my teaching career I could understand how a teacher (or student) could focus in on one thing at the complete exclusion of the other. I am sure Ed and I missed some equally teachable moments about geology when we were examining the invertebrate animals that morning.

Another time I met with Ed and some other faculty members right after I had attended a Math & Science Network video conference. I jokingly told my ASU peers how my Network boss, Gerry M., had commented during the video meeting that I looked like a movie actor. I said, "Gee, I am no actor." Ed retorted, "Steven, the hell you are not. Every day you get up in front of your class and act like you know what you are talking about."

What are friends for, I wondered?

The evening after the earlier mentioned science-math extravaganza featuring Bob Kansky, Alan McCormack and others, all of the presenters were invited to Ed and Joyce's house for cocktails. A couple of martinis on an empty stomach made me a little tipsy. As we were leaving I got mixed up and went up the stairs instead of down. Joyce called, "Steve, are you lost?"

I said, "No, I just wanted to see the bedroom where you two sleep."

It would have been much better had I admitted I was lost, confused, and lightheaded from drink.

Sometime in the mid 1990s when Ed and I were leading a workshop, I sensed he was miffed about something. When I asked him why, he replied, "Dammit, Steve, you didn't provide me with an outline of what we were to do."

I reminded him that every time we worked together he would deviate from the outline five minutes into the workshop. "I know it," he said, "but I have to have something in front of me that I can deviate from."

At our next workshop, I made sure there was an outline from which Ed could deviate.

Years later Ed and I were scheduled to do a workshop at 8:00 a.m. on a Saturday at the Catawba Science Center in Hickory. Instead of going together, Ed was to meet me there. Ed was not there at 8:00, which was so unlike him. I received a call not too much later from my wife saying that Ed had called her and wondered why I had not picked him up. Later that morning, Ed did appear and we worked smoothly together as we frequently had. Later in the afternoon, Ed said he wanted to lie down and that he was very tired. When the workshop was over, Ed asked me how to get home. He had driven the route hundreds of times. I thought he was kidding, but I also had some nagging thoughts that things were not right. The following Monday, I received a call from his wife, Joyce, saying that Ed had wrecked his truck on the trip home and that he was sick. A few days later we found out how sick—an inoperable brain tumor. Ed died a few months later. His death not only hurt his friends and loved ones, but it hurt the Center as well. I could never, thereafter, find anyone nearly as good to take his place. His untimely death was a blow to science teachers all over North Carolina. Whenever I visited a high school or middle school in the state and announced that I was from ASU, someone would invariably ask me if I knew Dr. Greene. When I said that he was my good friend, I knew I would be accepted at that school, plus I usually heard a funny story about Ed or how he had helped that person become a better teacher. I still miss him.

Another good science educator is Terry Carroll. Terry has a physics background and was frequently involved with the Center. In fact, he served as my Assistant Director for a while. Dr. Carroll knew a lot about solar energy and did workshops for sixth graders on electricity. Let me preface the next story by saying it occurred sometime in the late 1980s. Coincidentally, there was a popular movie and song sweeping the country called "Ghostbusters." When anything bad was about to occur, you were asked, "Who you gonna call?" and the answer was "Ghostbusters!" An important component of Terry's presentation was a section on safety. As a piece of advice, the kids were advised to call 911 if they saw a power line down, electrical appliances near water, etc. One time when Terry was wrapping up his program by asking what to do if students saw any inappropriate electrical situation, he asked a couple of guys who they were going to call? The answer they gave, of course, was

"Ghostbusters!"

A grant co-author and workshop presenter, Jeff Goodman, is undoubtedly the brightest guy I know. He is a Harvard grad, full of imagination and creativity, plus he is very humble. I have often accused him of having a photographic memory. The first day we met the 12 teachers and 24 girls who participated in the Women in Science program we went around the room and asked each person to introduce herself. Jeff then immediately repeated each of the 36 persons' names without error. Everyone was amazed. I think he may have used some sort of mnemonic device because at another program, two teachers walked in a couple of minutes late, and Jeff did not get their names. He asked me who they were, but I accidentally got the two mixed up giving one teacher the wrong first name and the second teacher the incorrect last name (possibly a reason no one has ever suggested that I had a photographic memory). Whenever Jeff did the name recall activity with this group, he would always give the two tardy teachers the incorrect names that I had originally given him, then say "Excuse me" and identify them both correctly. A major reason for the success of the Math and Science Education Center can be traced to great facilitators such as Jeff Goodman.

An ASU faculty member who contributed greatly to the success of the mathematics segment of the Center is Dr. William McGalliard. Bill is a mathematics educator and served as part-time MSEC Director from January to September 1985 when I arrived on the scene. He helped pave the way for me and got the Center off the ground. Bill's main claim to fame, from my point of view, is his work with schools in developing the Family Math program. He went out to the schools and spent an evening with teachers, students, their parents, siblings, and other relatives. Bill presented mathematical problems and challenges to the group, and each family would work together to try to solve the problem. There were all levels of difficulty of problems, something for everybody. Dr. McGalliard is a wonderful teacher and has the patience of Job. The Family

Math nights were well received and frequently were requested a second time by participating schools. One evening, right after Bill announced that the next math activity would be the last of the evening, a 6 or 7-year-old girl who was sitting near Dr. McGalliard began to cry. "Is she sick?" Bill asked the girl's mom.

"No," the mother replied, "she just doesn't want the evening to end. She is having so much fun."

If that isn't a fine tribute to a program and particularly the instructor, I don't know what is.

Another ASU mathematics professor who was a real Center trooper was Dr. Betty Long. Betty conducted many math hands-on workshops, particularly for elementary and middle school teachers. Her next door neighbor, Leslie Perry (Language Arts professor at a college in Tennessee) often teamed with her to do integrated math and literature workshops. Occasionally, I went along to add science activities to the mix. One time, just Betty and Leslie were going but neither had been to the Catawba Science Center in Hickory, the site of the workshop. Betty and I took a dry run down to the Catawba Science Center so she would know the way. The Hickory city layout is a bit confusing, and Betty said she wasn't sure where to turn to get to the Center. "At the flashing yellow light," I told her.

"But what if the light isn't flashing tomorrow?" she queried. "Turn there anyway," I gruffly responded.

She said that sounded OK with her. Obviously, the light was working the next day and the ladies did a great job.

Another time, I was to meet Betty and Leslie at a rural elementary school some distance from ASU. We drove separately, and I got lost. So did they. As chance would have it, we almost collided on a country road that turned out to be 20 miles from the school. What a coincidence! We asked a passing motorist the way to the school and finally wound up at our destination 45 minutes late. Leslie and Betty stayed at a motel that night, and everything went smoothly until the following day when ASU received a call from someone wondering why the two professors didn't check out of the motel that morning, and where was the room key, anyway? The only thing I could think of to tell the inn proprietors was that the two professors were so focused on doing a good job (which they did) that they couldn't think of anything else and, yes, the Center would pay the bill.

CHAPTER 11

Controversy

Over the very many years of my career, I haven't taught many concepts that students found objectionable. When I talk about sexual reproduction in humans, the class gets very quiet. There was the time I was discussing female reproductive anatomy and I wrote the word "vagina" on the blackboard. Some of the usually sleepy athletes in the back row showed some latent interest for a while; nothing ongoing, however. A couple of years back, a guy asked in class if "size matters." I truthfully told him that I had no idea. One time at a study group in an all-girls dorm we were discussing some birth control methods that were mentioned in the textbook, one of which was early withdrawal. A young lady asked me what that was. Another co-ed sort of saved the day by interjecting, "Don't worry, Dr. D., I'll explain that to her after you leave."

The other main topic of controversy is, of course, evolution. I don't want to step on anyone's religious convictions, but I do want students to be able to separate scientific data from faith. I tell students that evolution (change over time) is an integral part of understanding biology. I try to keep it factual but not threatening to students' belief systems. Back at Billings Senior High School, we had a self-paced biology program which utilized learning packets, one of which was entitled "Evolution." One year I had several Latter Day Saints (Mormons) in my classes, some of whom were my very best students. They came to me as a group and said they didn't mind doing the packet, but their parents would object to the word "evolution." I said "OK" and went through their packets and substituted the word "change" for "evolution" whenever the word appeared. The kids could see what I had done and they accepted it willingly, thanking me for doing it.

"Now we can take the packets home with us at night," one student said.

In this case it was the students who bridged the gap between science and religion.

In another episode, many years later, the end result was definitely not good. A student in my biology class at ASU told me in private that he objected to my lectures on evolution and that they ran counter to his religious beliefs. I tried to persuade him to keep the biology content separate from his religious views. I also told him that Darwin at one time was thinking of taking up the ministry, but the student did not believe me. Keep in mind that the young man, I'll call him Arthur, was a good kid and although upset by the situation was not angry with me. Later in the semester, a movie was playing that depicted the life of Jesus. Arthur wanted to know if I would go see it with him. He was surprised when I said that I would go. Unfortunately, things came up and we missed the movie. I think he earned a B in the course and we parted friends. Unfortunately, I got word that summer that Arthur had killed himself—that he was unhappy personally and was having trouble coming to grips with his beliefs. I have often wondered if things might have played out differently had I attended the Jesus movie with him. It would not have hurt me to make a greater effort to attend it with him. He was a good kid.

I'll close the topic on a lighter note. Early one semester I discussed what the early earth's atmosphere might have been like. I suggested that some of the earth's early life existed in an oxygen-free environment and that the food for these anarobes was probably some inorganic metallic compounds. When I asked a related question on a subsequent quiz, "What probably was the first food consumed by living organisms on earth?" one student responded: "An apple."

The controversy of education is not confined to biology courses. My son teaches psychology at the United States Air Force Academy and during one of his lectures was making the point that differences in animal sleeping times were probably evolutionary based. After class, a cadet asked what would be a good creationist explanation for differences in animal sleep time.

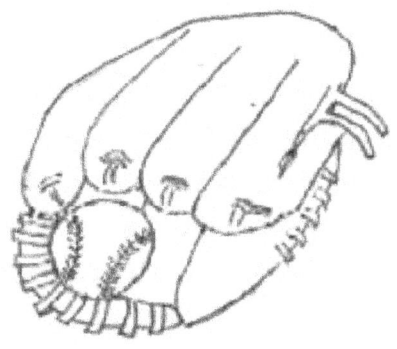

CHAPTER 12

Humor in Sports

Humor in education extends beyond the classroom to include the ball fields, gymnasium, locker room, stage, and anywhere else students gather for instruction. All of these places are extensions of the formal classroom; they are also places where learning and teaching take place. Some of my own athletic experiences illustrate this.

My first experience as a football player was a junior varsity game against our school's biggest rival, Central. Early in the game we were forced to punt. This presented a problem because Frank the punter had never before done that, nor had our center ever snapped the ball back to a kicker. Worse yet, Grover, a skinny kid, was sent in to block (protect) the punter, and he hadn't done that either. As luck would have it, the center hiked the ball a trifle low, Frank proceeded to bobble it and then attempted to kick it. All the while, the seemingly huge Central line was bearing down on Grover and Frank. Frank lifted his foot to kick just as a Central player lunged into Grover with such force that it knocked him backward at the exact same time that Frank's foot was moving forward.

Unfortunately, Frank's foot never made contact with the ball; it did, however, strike Grover's ass with such force that it sent him forward two or three yards—much further than the ball had moved. Coaches and teammates were very concerned about Central getting the ball deep in our territory. I was more concerned with Grover's behind, which he was now rapidly rubbing and which would soon be sporting a mammoth bruise the size of Texas. A comedian couldn't have dreamed up a funnier scenario. It turned out we won the game, and I even ran for a touchdown, but my main memory is that first futile attempt by our team to kick the ball.

My next year was spent on the Varsity squad as the team's quarterback. I wasn't very good, too small to play on the line, not quick enough for a running back or tough enough for any other position. We did have a much better player scheduled for the position, but he got hurt and was out for the season. The coach had to put me somewhere and the QB position was one where the coach could vent a lot of his hostility. So I played the position for the next three years, but never well. It was a small high school so there wasn't a lot of competition for the position. From my freshman to senior years, I went from 135 pounds to 146 pounds, a big improvement! Back in those days, working out with weights was not encouraged by most coaches.

I played quarterback and liked to throw passes (both during and after the game) but wasn't very successful either time. I usually got tackled for a loss before I could get rid of the ball. I had a slow release, coach said. In a game against the Eagles I dropped back to try a pass and was about to be tackled, so I just threw the ball in desperation. It hit one of the Eagles' defensive players in the helmet and bounced into the hands of one of our receivers, who had the coordination to react to the situation and scored our only touchdown of the game. Unfortunately, the "bouncing the ball off another player's helmet" strategy never worked again, although I did try it a few times.

In another game, I called play 28, which required the entire backfield to go to the right, including me. For some reason, between the time I called the play in the huddle and the time I got under the center to call signals, I forgot which play I had called. I thought I had said 49, which involved everyone going to the left. So while everyone else went right, I went left. Needless to say, I was tackled for a huge loss. At halftime, coach was livid. "I've never coached such a bunch of dummies. The quarterback calls a play and everybody else runs the wrong way. What the H is the matter with you guys?" he shouted.

I started to explain that I had made the mistake, but he was having none of it. "You shut up." he said. "If I want to hear anything from you, I'll ask you."

"But," I started before again being cut off.

It never occurred to him that he had a quarterback who couldn't remember, for even 10 seconds, what play he had just called.

Our team's biggest nightmare, and mine too, was a game against the Ponies. They were a much bigger school and their players were men. They were stronger, tougher, and much more experienced than we. I knew we were in trouble from the opening kickoff when I tried to tackle their kick return man and he knocked me backwards at least five yards, like a horse or cow brushing off a fly. His name was Mack something-or-other. I think Mack Truck, the way he ran over everyone. Several of our starters were injured, a couple seriously. At the half we trailed 34-0 and took a pretty good tongue lashing from coach. The next week I noticed a rash on my toes. I asked coach if he thought I had athlete's foot. He said, "No, I don't think you are good enough to get athlete's foot." Cruel, but probably true.

Speaking of coaches, the Ponies' mentor weighed roughly 300 pounds and was meaner than he was fat. He slugged one of his players for committing a penalty. He made our coach seem like a cream puff, both in size and gruffness. I did throw a touchdown pass to Larry (who was very fast), and I finally made a few tackles during the second half, but by then it was against their third or fourth team. We chatted with some of their players after the game, and they said the reason they were so tough besides being big, strong and fast is that they were more afraid of their coach than they were of the other team. If I ever had any confidence in my football abilities, I certainly lost them after the game with the Ponies.

One more humorous incident I believe shows our team's and my total ineptitude. First, a bit of signal calling background for those not familiar with the intricacy of the sport. On our team this is the way it worked: I would call a certain offensive play in the huddle, but when I got up to the line of scrimmage I had the option of changing the play based on how the defense was lined up. If I yelled out "red" I was telling the team that I was changing the play. Maybe the original play called in the huddle was 45, which was a running play. When I sized up the defense, I might decide that a short pass was better against that defensive lineup, so I would holler "red 66." Simple enough, right? One more detail to go with play calling is the snap number. In other words, on which number would the center hike the ball between his legs to the quarterback, who had his hands behind the center's butt to get the ball. I would first say the number of defensive linemen 4,5,6,7, 8, and then hut 1, hut 2, hut 3, hut 4etc. Obviously, if the play has been called on 3 that is when the center would snap the ball to me. Here is where it gets confusing. If I saw an 8 man defensive line, it meant to go to the automatic play—a short pass right over the line of scrimmage. Amazingly, it often worked. Remember, all I had to say to run this play was "8." Also, if at any time I thought the other team's defense was not ready, I could call a play on the "sound." This meant as soon as I opened my mouth to say anything, the center would snap the ball. We often tried it near the goal line or in other short yardage situations. Here comes the joke. During a game my senior year, we had gained nine yards on first down; a good time to call a play on the sound and get that first down, I thought. So, a running play on the sound was called; however, when I got up to the line of scrimmage I saw the defense lined up in an 8-man line. Remembering the automatic 8 while entirely forgetting that I had called the original play on the sound, I was not ready for the ball to be hiked, in fact, I don't think I had yet put my hands "under center." I called out "8." Whoa, Wilbur, the center, snapped the ball firm and hard. With my hands not there to receive it, the football sailed maybe 20 feet straight into the air. No one, and I mean no one—players, coaches, fans, referees, nobody—had any idea where the ball was or how it happened, except for me. The ball came down in my arms, almost as if I had passed it to myself. Of course, I was tackled for a huge loss. My goof up represented just another situation when we didn't make first down when we should have. When Wilbur asked me what had happened, I tried to tell him but it didn't seem to make any sense. Even when I went over to hardboiled coach to explain he just said, "I don't want to know."

To this day, I often wake up in the night laughing about that extreme screw-up that I made and the confused looks on everyone's faces. It was almost as if I had a secret that no one else knew anything about.

Basketball also lent itself to some humorous situations. One year our team was led by one of Montana's greatest Native American athletes, Larry Pretty Weasel. During a tournament game with our rival Central Rams, Larry had the ball at the top of the key and all of a sudden it was whistling toward my face. I was wide open but didn't even know it. Luckily, I caught the ball on the move, but to avoid traveling, I had to shoot the ball immediately. I shot the ball so hard it caromed off the backboard with such force that it came all the way back to where Larry was standing. He didn't often get mad but did say, "Steve, Steve—wake up."

Earlier in that same game, another Native American, Donald "Lucky" Dreamer, came up to me after I was called for traveling. Lucky seldom criticized me or any of his other teammates, but this time said, "Steve, that is the third time you have traveled."

I responded, "No, it was the first time I was called for the violation."

"Yes, you have been called for traveling once, but you have actually traveled almost every time you have had the ball. You are moving your feet all over the place. Wake up, Steve."

With all the wake up advice from my teammates, you would think I had not gone to bed the previous evening. And yes, we won the game in overtime to take third place. I suffered a severe leg cramp just as the overtime period began, and I did not finish the game. Some of my critics credit my injury and not playing in the critical overtime period for our victory.

One other semi-humorous story about that season involved our Center, Robert Little Light, nicknamed Chief or Goose (for Goose Tatum of Globetrotter fame.) Bob usually didn't have much to say. He spoke more through his actions on the court, but the following incident still makes me smile. We were playing the Eagles, the three time defending state champs. In the game earlier in the season up at their place, they thumped us pretty good, but playing them at home presented a whole different perspective. Larry was hot and the Eagles were missing one of their players. Late in the game we had a one-point lead when I saw a crack in their defense and drove for the basket. Too late I saw the Eagles big center underneath the basket. In mid air I thought I could still get the shot off and by twisting my body, avoid charging into their big man. I did make the shot but, unfortunately, crashed into their center. The basket counted, but I was called for a foul. I was angry with myself for making the foul. They will just make two free throws and we won't be any better positioned than before I drove in, I thought, still disgusted by my foul. While I was busy muttering about my error in judgment, Little Light said "nice shot." When I didn't respond, he said much louder, "nice shot." I still was talking to myself when I heard Bob say "Dammit, Steve, I said nice shot."

I finally broke through my stupor and offered a weak, "Thanks, Bob."

It was funny in that not only was it one of the few times he ever acknowledged one of my plays, it was the first and only time I heard Goose swear during a game. I'm sure he had some bad words for me in Crow from time to time, but I'll never know. Next to Larry, I think he was our best player.

The big Eagle center missed the free throw and we got the ball back and hung on to win. It was the only time during my high school career that we beat the Eagles.

Our basketball team my senior year was a joke with the graduation of Larry, Dreamer, and Little Light. My friend, Wilbur, and I were to lead the squad, as we were the only regulars returning from last year's great team. The problem was that neither of us could bring our A game with us on the same night. When Wilbur was on,

I'd be off and vice versa. We won only a handful of games all season and generally stunk—that is, until tournament time.

Then, for some inexplicable reason, we got hot and played like the better Hardin Bulldog teams of yore. We barely lost our first game, but then won three straight to earn a spot in the consolation championship game, just like last year. One of the wins was over the host G.F. Central Mustangs, a team we had never before beaten on their home court. Another victory came at the expense of the hated Central Rams. In that game we led from 3-5 points most of the game; Wilbur and I were hot as was our Native American center, Lloyd Old Coyote. As most fans in the gym expected, the Rams caught us with 44 seconds left in the game. With 10 seconds remaining, we trailed by two, but this time luck was on our side. I nailed a 15-foot jump shot to tie the game. When Central threw the ball away at the other end of the court, only 4 seconds remained. I held the ball out of bounds until time ran out.

Years later, Coach Casey was still telling anyone who would listen about what a heads up play I had made by not chancing an interception of a thrown in pass under the Central basket. A real thinking man's play, he would say. Now, here is where the humor comes in. The reason I held the ball out of bounds was not that I feared risking an interception on any slight chance to score we might have, but because I thought we led by a point and had won the game! I never told coach otherwise. Unless he reads this, he will never know the difference. I hope no one tells him either—I still like the praise, even though it wasn't deserved.

In the overtime, I scored the only two field goals made by either team. When taking both shots, the basket looked larger than a fat man's bathtub. I thought there was no way I could miss and I didn't. So we beat the Rams at the State Tournament in overtime for the second year in a row. That, in itself, to Bulldog fans, is very humorous. The next day I was named to the All Tournament starting five by UPI. More humor. It was all a big mistake. My teammate Wilbur deserved it more than I. He scored more points, was scrappier, and a bit more competitive (also smarter; he is a successful orthopedic surgeon in Bellingham, Washington.) I was more show than substance. My dad used to like to say I looked better missing a free throw or lay-up than anyone else he knew. He wasn't being funny, either. A week or so after the tournament, I received a letter from the coach at a nearby college offering me a scholarship to play basketball and baseball. My now overly inflated ego would not let me turn it down. More about that in the section under college humor.

A basketball witticism from my college days follows:

Our first games were Thanksgiving weekend and they were out of state. We took the train at 1:00 a.m. and arrived at our destination about noon. We were playing the Savages (yes, they have bowed to political correctness and have since changed their nickname). Anyway, as luck would have it, the scoreboard quit early in the second half so the score was kept on a big blackboard. I was sitting at the end of the bench—the closest team member to the blackboard. Coach Herb sat at the other end of the bench, farthest from the makeshift scoreboard. Herb, by the way, had the unflattering nickname of McGoo (after the nearly blind cartoon character). He definitely could not see well and admittedly the blackboard score was difficult to read at best. It is true that when he called "Dyche!" I thought he wanted me to go into the game so I proceeded to take off my warm up jacket. "Come here," he said. He squinted at me and asked, "What is the score?" Then, "Sit back down." I got the big guffaw from my teammates and weakly stammered that I at least knew the score—but obviously only the score of the game.

Montana public schools do not sponsor boy's baseball at any level; winters are too long and springs too short in this northern state to allow for much scheduled outdoor spring activities. However, many communities do sponsor Little League (ages 7-12), Babe Ruth (ages 13-15), and American Legion (ages 16-18) baseball during the summer. I participated at all of those levels. My early baseball experiences were checkered. I could field the ball fairly well, but I could not hit. I invariably struck out when I was at bat. Sometime between my 11th and 12 birthdays I started to mature and experienced a big growth spurt. By the time I was 12, I weighed 130 lbs and was 5' 7" tall—a head or two taller than many of my younger baseball teammates. I also discovered that I could pitch.

Being considerably stronger, bigger and faster than anyone else in the league, I dominated. Looking back at the team pictures of 1952 and '53 I am embarrassed by how much larger I was than everyone else. I got a lot of publicity for throwing no hitters and for having a high batting average, but I should have done those things—I was shaving while some of my opponents were barely able to tie their shoes and zip up their pants. Babe Ruth ball was a little more difficult—other boys were becoming men, so the competition was tougher. Still, I threw some shut outs and got my share of base hits. My best friend, Frankie, was my catcher and was quite good. By the time I was old enough for Legion ball I was probably just average size, if that. I had some success but nothing like my no-hitters of Little League times. Our Legion team barely won half of its games, yet we had the best record in town history. There were some humorous moments that I will now share with you.

This one I like to call "The guy who would not be walked." When I was in my last year of Babe Ruth ball (ages 13-15) we were playing against one of our rival teams from Laurel. This team always gave us fits and we rarely beat them. But in this particular game we had a one-run lead going into the next to last inning. I was pitching, and we had two men out and they had a runner on first base. Laurel's best hitter was up to bat, and I had a long history of not being able to get him out. I called our catcher, Frankie, and our coach out to the mound and said I wanted to walk this guy (his name was Huck) and pitch to the next batter who was, in my opinion, a much easier out. Our coach said he didn't like the idea of putting the go-ahead run on base, but it was OK if I felt that strongly about it. So Frankie stepped outside from the plate and I threw an obvious Ball one, outside; then the same thing, Ball two, outside. Then, for some reason that maybe escaped even Huck, on the third pitch he stepped close to home plate, extended his arms and swung mightily at the ball. Of course, the ball was too far outside to hit, so strike one on the batter. Well, the Laurel coach was livid. His face got beet red and veins started sticking out on his neck.

"Huck!" he screamed, "What in the h—do you think you are doing? Don't ever swing at a pitch when they are trying to walk you! I don't care if the next pitch is right down the middle of the plate, you are not to swing at it."

"Time out!" I shouted. Frankie came running out to the pitcher's mound. I suggested to Frankie that we now pitch to Huck.

"We know he won't swing at the next pitch so he will have Strike two on him, and then maybe we can get him out," I said.

Frankie wasn't convinced. "What will coach say?"

I responded that if we could get Huck out we would probably win the game, and coach would be happy. So the next pitch I fired right down the middle. Huck dutifully followed orders and did not swing—Strike two. Again, a conference with Frankie; we could still hear the Laurel coach berating Huck. Frankie called for a curve ball; some days I had a pretty good one, and this was one of those days. I fired my best curve at Huck, and he obviously was still gun shy about swinging and he let the ball go past. "Strike three," the umpire roared. Laurel went out harmlessly in the last inning—the intended walk that backfired on them seemed to take the starch out of their collars, and we were finally able to beat them. Neither our coach nor our dads were as happy about the no-walk decision as Frankie and I were. We were scolded for not following through with the decision to walk Huck. Still, that night, I overheard my dad laughingly tell the story to my mom. If no one else thought so, Frankie and I found the entire episode to be hilarious. Laurel players, coaches, and fans may not have agreed.

When I was 14, I pitched a shutout against the PC Panthers, but some of the luster of the game came off when after hitting a single, I got picked off of first—caught napping. After getting the hit, I was mugging it up with my teammates and lost track of where the ball was. When I stepped off the base to take my lead, the PC first baseman immediately tagged me out. The old hidden ball trick! I would have liked to crawl under the base. Instead, I walked sheepishly back to the dugout enduring the catcalls of the PC home fans. The best game I pitched that year, or ever maybe, was against the Laurel team I described earlier. I threw five perfect innings, walked a man in the 6th, then gave up a hard single in the 7th to guess who—Huck. No wonder I didn't want to pitch to him the next year in that game with them that I described earlier. After Huck's hit and a stolen base, the next batter bunted the ball in front of home plate. Frankie grabbed the ball and promptly threw it into left field as the winning run came in to score. We lost 1-0.

My most exciting inning occurred a couple of years later in a Legion game against (you guessed it) Laurel. We did play several teams other than Laurel but the best "stuff " seemed to take place in games with them. Johnny S. was pitching for us that game and we had a 3-0 lead going into the top of the 4th inning. Johnny had some control problems and gave up some walks and a couple of hits, and Laurel was able to tie the score 3-3 after two men were out. They still had bases loaded when our coach, Joe, brought me in to pitch in relief. Johnny went back to his former position of shortstop. My first pitch was hit very hard—but right at Johnny who fielded the ball cleanly and stepped on second for the force out, getting himself and our team out of a major jam. I had lucked out of the inning by throwing just one pitch. It turned out I was our first batter in the bottom of the same inning. In my first time up I had hit the ball hard, but got under it so much that it resulted in a high pop up to the third baseman. Now, it was my next at bat. First pitch was ball one. Then, I got the same pitch that I had earlier popped up, a waist high fast ball. I swung hard and the ball flew off my bat. I started sprinting toward first when I heard my dad say, "Go all the way, Steve", then "slow down, it is out of here". The ball must have traveled well over 400 feet and I had an easy home run. It must have been the bat because it never happened again.

I remember two scary situations from my baseball days. One involved a collision between the catcher and third baseman of the visiting team. They were chasing a foul pop up and neither of them heard the other call for the ball. They hit hard, with the catcher going into seizures and losing consciousness. Of course, there was no doctor and it was a Sunday. The game was held up for at least an hour while some fans tried to locate the town's sawbones. I was really worried about the two boys, particularly the catcher. Finally, the MD showed up, stepped over the more severely injured player and loudly announced, it looks like rain to me. That broke the tension; both boys recovered and were not seriously injured.

The other scary baseball incident, with humor, involves a pitcher from the Cougars, named Big Al. The Cougar team was pretty good to begin with and when they added Big Al to their roster, they became almost unbeatable. Big Al looked like he was 30 years old. He had a beard, scars around his eyes, and a generally mean countenance about him. Reportedly, he had been kicked out of high school for beating up classmates; he also supposedly had a brush with the law. Besides that, he was big; maybe 6'2" tall and weighed about 200 pounds. He wasn't quite yet 18, but as I say, he looked 30. He was the team's ace pitcher and to add to the rumor mill, he reportedly split a kid's head open when he hit him in the noggin with one of his patented fast balls. The story goes that he laughed when it happened. Needless to say, some of my teammates and I were not real excited about batting against Big Al. Minutes before our first game with them, we were in awe as we saw him warming up. You could hear the ball pop clear across the field as Al's pitches exploded into the catcher's mitt. I was playing center field that game and hitting fifth in the batting lineup. In the first inning, Big Al struck out the side. My turn to bat came in the second inning. My palms were sweating and my knees were knocking. The first pitch I didn't even see—it was a fast ball and it sounded like it was right over the plate. The second pitch the same thing (after all, this guy could throw 90 miles per hour pitches). Big Al could easily have struck me out with another fastball; instead he struck me out with a curve ball. I badly stepped in the bucket and missed the pitch by a couple of feet. My next at bat was the same sequence of pitches and the same result. In the outfield I did make a good running catch on a long fly ball hit by Big Al. I hoped it didn't make him too mad. Our team trailed 5-0 going into the last inning. We managed a hit and two walks—coupled with some errors by the Cougars, we were able to close the gap to 5-3. When I came up to bat again, we had runners on first and second and only one man out. Our coach remembered my previous times at the plate with Big Al, so he called for me to sacrifice bunt. I was a decent bunter and had some success in my career in advancing runners by bunting and even occasionally beating one out for a base hit. I can do this, I thought as big Al entered his wind up. Sure enough, another high, fast one. I squared around into my bunting stance and tried to get my bat on the ball. I think Big Al's fastballs tended to rise a bit on their way to the plate. My bat made contact with the ball but I just got the very underside of the ball. It shot up and made a high parabola shaped arc toward third base. It was one of the highest pop flies I had ever hit. In fact, it was a fly ball and the umpire invoked the "infield fly rule" and I was immediately called out. A real rarity—being called out on the infield fly rule on a bunt (batter is automatically out on an infield fly when there are runners on first and second base or first, second, and third and less than two men out).

We lost the game, but good news—when we played the Cougars at their field, Big Al was not pitching. I wanted to win the game but thought if we had too much success against this other pitcher, they would bring in Big Al—heaven forbid. Later that summer, Big Al signed to play professionally in the Pioneer rookie league. Still later, we heard he had run afoul of the law again. I will always remember that game because it is when I learned one thing about good baseball pitching—that I could not hit it!

CHAPTER 13

◆

Campus Humor

Earlier, I mentioned that I accepted a scholarship at a nearby college to play basketball and baseball. The school is called Rocky Mountain College. It was a small (400 students) liberal arts college and was church related. The school had a reputation for producing athletic coaches and ministers. I never was a religious person, but I really didn't mind the required weekly chapel or the two Bible classes that were mandatory. It didn't hurt me any and it was a learning experience. I mention the college's religious background only to set the scene for some freshman humor. That fall, our dormitory was to have a float in the homecoming parade. Our advisor was a retired Methodist minister who enjoyed a good laugh. He and some others arranged for a local seamstress to make a cow costume with an enormous udder. Attached to the cow was a sign that read, "We've got the game in the bag." My friend John and I were to be inside the costume—I was the front and he the back. I jokingly kidded him that I thought of him more of a horse's behind than a cow's. Anyway, I guess the udder flopped around shamelessly as our float followed the parade route through the streets of downtown.

The following week we heard that our float originally won first prize, but the float was disqualified for not being dignified enough for a church supported school. I found that odd in that we had a retired minister as an adviser. Two of the judges were professors of mine and I thought the ruling, disqualifying the udder float, was ridiculous. Is there something sac-religious about a cow's udder, I wondered? It is the universal gland of all mammals. Was it immoral to drink milk? After all, it came from a cow's udder. My senior year, the dormitory entered the float a second time and with the exact same result and subsequent disqualification. No one could accuse Rocky of being progressive. I was furious—I was OK with the Bible classes and the required chapel attendance, but this "udder" decision was extremely Victorian and a turn off for most of the school's students. It was an "utter" catastrophe. It was, to my way of thinking, stupid. Anyway, the float to most people was humorous and deserved that first place award.

At Rocky, there were lots of college pranks and I participated in a few of them. Once, with the help of about eight guys, we lifted a student's Volkswagon Beetle that was parked in a straight-in slot and turned the car 90 degrees so it was wedged between adjacent cars. Consequently, it could not move forward or backward.

My roommate and I were also prank victims. The doors on our dorm rooms opened inward, so mischievous John in the room next door would prop coke bottles full of water against our door, then knock and run. My roommate or I would then open the door and promptly flood our room with the pop bottle's water contents. After a few such episodes, I slipped into John's room and hid some recently purchased Limburger cheese under his steam radiator. Whew, did it ever stink that night when the heat came on. John accused a nemesis down the hall and I got off scot free, for a while anyway. Another time when I was the sole prankster, the joke involved my closest friends. John, my roommate, Dale, and a couple of other guys from our dorm worked in the food kitchen and had to report to work in the cafeteria a half hour before dinner was served. For some reason they never seemed to know what time it was so they would ask me. I am pretty much time driven so I usually knew the time of day. One cold late winter afternoon, I got the "what time is it" question. Feeling devilish, I said I'd get my watch and find out. On my way to the room to get my watch, I noticed that the dormitory lounge was empty and that the clock read 4:30 PM. I quickly set the time up to 5:30 and did the same to my watch. I saw my friend Richard and told him to set his watch up one hour. When he asked why, I told him I was doing an experiment on estimating time passage. I ran downstairs where the kitchen crew guys were playing ping-pong.

"Hey fellas", I announced, "it's almost 5:30!"

"Geez, we better go," Dale said. John stopped and commented that it could not be that late.

"Look in the lounge or ask somebody else," I suggested.

"Oh, here is Richard. Hey, he's got 5:30 on his watch, too. Let's go." They all ran out into the winter cold one hour early. I had a real laugh until Richard spilled the beans later that night, For some reason, some of my "friends" weren't speaking to me for a while. Well, at least they didn't ask me the time anymore.

CHAPTER 14

◆

College Sports Humor

After a couple of days on campus I wandered over to the gymnasium—after all, I was an athletic recruit. A pick-up basketball game was being played by 10 guys, all of whom seemed much better than I. The game was being dominated by a big, black man named William, a junior college transfer out of Chicago. I was intimidated by all of these bigger and what appeared to be better players. I later played for a few minutes in a 2 on 2 game and did OK, but I got winded after only a short while. I heard someone refer to me as "fat boy". It was then that I ran into Coach Herb.

"Dyche," he said, "I didn't know I had recruited such a fat guy."

I had worked for my grandparents that summer and put on about 15 pounds, primarily from eating rich southern cooking (my grand folks were from Kentucky before they migrated to Montana). Some of the weight gain might have been muscle, but most was flab around the waist. So I began a running program to get back in shape. I lost a few pounds and regained some endurance, but I always remained a little chubby after that. I also had lost some speed and I didn't really ever get back in the shape I had been in during high school. The Rocky gym was small and Herb eventually combined varsity and jv's for practice so about one third of us were sitting out at any one time. Bottom line, I didn't work off much weight during practice. I weighed 160 at the end of the season—about 10 pounds more than the year before. The first two weeks of practice I was relegated to the junior varsity, but then after a scrimmage game against the varsity, which we almost won, I moved up to the varsity and stayed there for the season.

I mentioned earlier our season's first game against the Savages and the scoreboard incident with coach Herb. Inexplicably, the next night I did actually get into the game. I hadn't been in 15 seconds when the ball came to me and I had an open shot. Just off the rim, darn it. A minute or two later, another opportunity for a shot—bingo I had made my first collegiate basket. Then, seconds before the end of the half—a fast break opportunity, a perfect pass from Big William and I hit another short jumper. At half time, even intimidating William said it was a good shot, The second half was a bit of a downer. I scored another basket but I became very tired and I made three quick fouls trying to guard my man. I was too excited and very nervous. I'd bet my heart was beating 200 times/minute. I had to come out of the game. I was just exhausted. Herb grumbled something about not being in shape. Unlike the first night, we lost the game, but I think we should have won both games. So did McGoo. He said we thought we were a bunch of pros but we sure didn't play like it.

"You don't mean pros, Herb," Big William said, "you mean a bunch of prophylactics!"

I didn't see much action after that. I did start in a big benefit game—I don't know why. I didn't do anything except miss a couple of shots. I did have a couple of good practices, though. On the last night of practice before the district tournament, Herb had to narrow the squad to 10 players, so he had a scrimmage game lined up amongst the 14 or 15 guys vying for a slot on the traveling team (which also meant you earned your letter). A week or so earlier I had dislocated my thumb. Casual Frank, the assistant coach, had taped it up in a way that made it slightly difficult to handle the ball, but for some reason made my shot release much smoother and I was shooting great. During this last scrimmage I couldn't miss and made 7 or 8 baskets. McGoo blew the whistle.

"Next basket wins," he announced.

"Next basket my eye," I shouted. "We are 10 points ahead of the starters."

"Next basket wins," he repeated.

Big William said, "I am going to guard this little farmer, Dyche." He called me farmer as a mark of complete disdain. Well, he did guard me tough. He was so big and strong. Finally, I got the ball took a step backwards and just threw the ball at the basket—way too hard. But wait, it hit the backboard and bounced through the goal. The scrubs beat the varsity.

Later, Herb started announcing the traveling squad to the tournament. He named nine players, then slowly added "and.... Dyche". Yea, I thought. Unfortunately, we lost our first game at the tourney, but played for third and fourth the next night. In this last game of the season, in the Regional Tournament, our starting all conference guard, Tom, got in foul trouble late in the first half and I replaced him. Then, right after the half, he fouled out. I played the rest of he game and scored two baskets. More importantly, I held the man I was guarding scoreless.

The next week at a high school tournament, I introduced Herb to my mom. He evidently said something favorable about my play in the tournament. Her reply was that I always had been a good tournament player. A better assessment of my abilities came when Herb talked to each player about his relative strengths and weaknesses.

"Dyche," he began. "I am not afraid to put you in a game—you never hurt us. On the other hand, you don't help us much either." I thought it was an honest and fair evaluation of my talents. I am sure I could have been on the team the next three years and maybe started some, but I decided I had played my last game. Besides, I enjoyed my studies and spending time with a cheerleader girlfriend. I still rooted hard for Rocky and attended all home games and a couple of road games as well. I was very proud when the Rocky Bears captured the national NAIA championship last spring. McGoo would have loved it—even if he could not have read the scoreboard.

Baseball is more of an equalizer than basketball or football in terms of size and power and speed. Not that those attributes aren't important in baseball, they are, but you can still be a good player without them. A catcher, for example, need not be speedy, a pitcher doesn't have to be muscular, and a fielder doesn't have to be big. On our basketball team I was the shortest and lightest player (although in a couple of cases not by much). None of the teams we played had anyone smaller, either. Although Black Hills State had a guard my height, he was far more muscular. He was kind of like me—he didn't help his team much, either. On one road trip some of the home team fans thought I was the team mascot. It was understandable, my teammates called me Cub and our team name was the Bears. Not so, baseball—there were several guys on our team as well as the opposing teams who were about my size and build.

I was the starting pitcher the first game of the season down in Wyoming. I did Ok and we led after 6 innings. Herb took me out, it was cold and he didn't want me to hurt my arm, I guess. The trouble was our relief pitcher couldn't get anyone out and we lost the game. That was the closest I would ever get to being a winning collegiate pitcher. Like basketball, my baseball career at Rocky started fast but went up in smoke in a hurry. In a double header against Black Hills, I had the embarrassing distinction of being the losing pitcher in both games. One humorous situation, I recall, occurred in the second game of the twin bill. I was pitching with the bases loaded. The batter hit the ball hard right back at me and all I could do was put my glove up. The ball ripped the glove off my hand and carried it almost to second base while the ball trickled into the outfield. Black Hills runners were scurrying around the bases giving BH three more runs. Needless to say, I didn't pitch much after that.

During practice one day, we were shagging balls in the outfield. Herb hit a fly ball, ostensibly to me, but he didn't hit it very well. It was short and quite a bit to my left, but I started running for it anyway. I think the wind must have held the ball up a bit. I dove for it and the ball lodged in the webbing of my glove just before it would have hit the ground. It probably was the best catch of my life. Herb, in McGoo style asked, "who caught that?"

"It was Dyche," someone said. I am not saying Coach Herb was easily impressed, but I started in centerfield for the rest of the season.

In a game against the Pioneers, I swung mightily at a pitch, but barely topped the ball. It dribbled out in front of home plate just out of easy reach for the catcher. The pitcher sort of stumbled and did not get to the ball either. My first college base hit. The ball didn't travel 25 feet. Pitiful, I thought, but I'll take it. In the double header loss to Black Hills (described earlier), I did drive the ball all the way to the left field fence but their outfielder caught it. It wasn't all that impressive—there was a strong wind blowing out. The next batter hit a home run in about the same place.

Our last scheduled game was against our inter-city rivals, the Big E Yellow jackets. It was the third game between us, each team had won one. The winner would advance to the conference tournament. My first at bat came with men on second and third base. I swung late but hit a line drive into right field, driving in 2 runs; my first RBI's of the season. My second time up I hit a pitch into left field, driving in another run. The third time up I hit a hard smash but the shortstop gloved it, but couldn't make the throw to first. In the last inning the score tied, Herb wanted someone to pinch-hit for me. I told him I was 3 for 3 and to please let me bat. He did and I hit a line drive to left field. They were playing me deep—Lord knows why, and the left fielder caught the ball. It was my last at bat in organized ball. We lost 13-12. The next spring I came down with a terrible sore arm and did not play. My junior and senior years were devoted more to studies, the cheerleader and a new girl. Although I never really played organized ball again, I watched my son and daughter, my grandchildren and friends play a variety of sports. I now coach, referee and umpire—all from the grandstand or bleachers. I must have learned a lot while playing because now—I never make a mistake, either coaching or officiating.

Briefly going back to sports humor in the classroom, I want to mention a story about three ASU basketball players enrolled in my biology class. One semester, fairly early in my tenure at Appalachian

State, I had three basketball players and a cheerleader in my biology section. They all sat in the back corner hoping to attract as little of my attention as possible. To encourage class discussion, I throw out some relatively easy questions to get things going. The three ball players were named Tige, Kareem, and Jeremy. One day I asked Tige a question I thought he would be able to answer. Here is the dialogue from that session:

Dyche: "Tige, could you please answer that question?" Tige: "I'll pass to Kareem."
Kareem: "I'll pass to Jeremy." Jeremy: "I'll pass back to Tige."
Dyche: "You know, if you guys would have passed the basketball as well and as often as you passed your turn to answer the question, our team might have won a few more games this season."
Class: Much laughter.

    The three players were adequate students while the cheerleader was considerably more studious. One day I told her that she was out performing the three ball players in class and that she was much more pleasant to look at. She responded, "I don't consider either comment to be much of a compliment!" She, of course, said it loudly enough so that all three of the players could hear. Again, lots of class laughs. The three roundballers were good sports and very nice young men.

    Next, some coach related stories at ASU. Early in our time at the university, Dona befriended the basketball coach's wife and we got complimentary tickets to all home games for years. Although she was a wonderful friend to Dona and a very nice person, she wasn't always tuned into sports. One of our rival schools had identical twin basketball players. When she asked her husband (our coach) how to tell them apart; referring to their numbered jerseys, he replied that Ron was 21 and Don was 23. "Oh," she exclaimed, "I thought twins had to be the same age."

    We later lived next door to a new coach who, it turned out, had been Michael Jordan's college roommate. I'm sure Michael was a guest at the coach's home sometime when we lived there. Too bad he didn't come over; I could have showed him a few moves. We also live in the neighborhood of ASU's three-time national champion football coach. He has given me a ride home on occasion, and I have given him some tips on how to be a successful football coach (are you kidding)! All three of these coaches were super-nice gentlemen. I couldn't help contrasting them with the Ponies' high school football coach of some 50 years ago.

Roger C, a New Mexico physical education teacher and coach, tells this story: A beginning class of high school tennis players were to have a singles tournament at the end of the school term. Players were to go to the gym where they would find the tournament brackets posted for the first round. Each participant was to find his/her opponent and play a match before the next week's class period. Later, Roger found one young man aimlessly pacing around the gym, apparently in some distress. "I can't find the guy I am supposed to be playing," he said.

"Well, describe him," suggested Roger.

"I can't," the young man said. "I don't even know him. All I know is that his last name is Bye." (Well, I said they were beginners.)

In a related story, in Roger's school, students began the term with a registration period during which they were to go to each faculty member's office and get the teacher's consent to take a particular class. An English as a Second Language student came by Roger's office and said he couldn't find one of his instructors. "Who is it?" asked Roger.

"I don't know if it is a man or woman," the student replied, "all I know is that the person's name is Staff."

CHAPTER 15

Some Final Thoughts and Stories

A former Long Island elementary school teacher, Ms. Dorothy H., shared this story with me. The teacher taught first grade, and her goal with her class that year was to get the youngsters to stop using baby talk. She pointed out to her students that they were no longer babies—that they were in the first grade now and they should try to talk a bit more like grown-ups. One day, early in the academic year, the teacher asked the students to share with the class something fun that they had done the past summer—and no baby talk. Here is the dialogue from that lesson:

Teacher: Mary, you can be first.
Mary: Ok, well, my parents and I got on the choo-choo train.
Teacher: Mary, remember, no baby talk.
Mary: My parents and I got on the train.
Teacher: That is much better.
Teacher: Alice, you are next.

HUMOR IN THE CLASSROOM

Alice: My mommy and daddy went out west to a dude ranch and we rode horsies.
Teacher: Alice, try it again—this time with no baby talk.
Alice: My mother and father and I went to a dude ranch out west and rode horses.
Teacher: Very good, Alice. Johnny, it is your turn. What did you do this summer?
Johnny: Well, I didn't do nothin' much.
Teacher: Well, you must have done something.
Johnny: Well, we went to this movie about a bear.
Teacher: ...and what was the bear's name?
Johnny: Ummm, Winnie, Winnie the, Winnie the, Winnie the shit!

Well, at least Johnny didn't get into trouble with his teacher by breaking into baby talk.

Jeff Goodman likes to recall this science-related story about a super ball and liquid nitrogen. Jeff had been asked by a middle school principal to do some science demonstrations for some of his classes. Jeff historically had done a demonstration using a super ball in the classroom. He would bounce it on the floor a few times, then he would pour liquid nitrogen on the ball and slam it to the floor. The ball would make a loud noise and shatter into a thousand pieces. But on this particular day, he was running low on liquid nitrogen so he used a smaller than usual portion of this extremely cold liquid. He poured what he had left on the ball and slammed it to the floor. Unfortunately, the ball, although very cold, did not shatter when it hit the floor but bounced all the way to the ceiling—breaking one of the classroom lights in the process. The students thought it was all planned and laughed uproariously. Jeff, science educator that he is, recovered enough to explain that sometimes science doesn't work as expected.

A mathematics educator with computer application expertise, Dr. Debbie Crocker, was conducting a hands-on technology workshop for high school teachers one evening. The topic was the use of probes that can be attached to graphing calculators to measure and graph such things as pH, decibels of sound, temperature, and even heart rate. While working with the heart rate probes, Dr. Crocker suggested that it might be nice to get a starting point heart rate of a "volunteer" and then pump caffeine into the test subject fairly often over a short period of time to see if and how it affected that person's heart rate. Since the workshop participants had already consumed either some coffee or cola drinks, Debbie wanted to draft someone who had not and normally did not partake of these beverages. She looked at me and saw "sucker" written all over my face. She knew that I normally did not drink coffee or carbonated beverages. So with a big smile on her face she strapped the heart rate probe and monitor on me at 6:00 p.m. and found my heart rate to be 64 beats per minute. "I am in good shape," I bragged, "I jog regularly, am athletic and I doubt if the caffeine will have any effect on me."

A few minutes past 6:00 p.m., Dr. Crocker had me choke down a cup of regular coffee and part of another. A half hour later, a glass of iced tea was forced on me. Still later, a bottle of some highly caffeinated soda pop was administered, and just before 9:00 p.m. I consumed another bottle, but only after I was repeatedly told that I was doing all of this for science. I noticed that I was becoming shaky and a bit irritable (more so than normal even). Also, I kept having to go to the men's room. A little after 9:00 in the evening, Debbie slapped the heart rate probe back on me. This time my heart rate was a whopping 136. Sure, part of this increase may have come from the excitement of the workshop and possibly some anticipation of the results. Yet the workshop participants, Dr. Crocker, and I all became believers that caffeine is a pretty strong stimulant—me more than the others, as I hardly slept a wink and had to get up and "go" several times during the night. On a bit more positive note, it was the first and only time that I was ever able to help Dr. Crocker with one of her technology workshops.

Judy S., a Watauga County elementary teacher who has won about every science teaching award there is, tells this story. A teaching mate had a pair of hamsters as pets in her classroom. One day she told Judy that there was something wrong with one of the hamsters and would she please take a look at the ailing rodent.

Judy said she would take a look but that she was definitely not an animal doctor. After a couple of days, Judy returned the animal and commented that she could find nothing wrong with it. "What about those two bumps below the abdomen?" the other teacher asked. Judy replied, "I believe those are testicles." "Yes," the other teacher replied, "but the other hamster doesn't have those bumps." Evidently a crash course in animal sex education was in order for this teacher.

Another teacher friend of Judy's wanted to borrow some of her frog eggs that Judy had ordered and placed in her aquarium. Judy obliged and gave her some of the developing eggs. She was quite surprised when a couple of days later the teacher friend excitedly announced that her maturing embryos now had legs. Judy thought that quite odd in that they were from the same batch of eggs and Judy's embryos showed no sign of leg buds. "Let me have a look," Judy said. She then exclaimed, "Those strands hanging down are not legs, that is fecal material from the embryos." Here again, a basic course in animal biology might have been appropriate for Judy's teacher friend.

Although I usually enjoy getting them, I have learned over the years to take student compliments with a grain of salt. A classic example took place recently in a downtown clothing store. My wife and I were in the men's department looking for something for our son's birthday. The young clerk eyed me and asked, "Aren't you Dr. Dyche?" After I said I was, he introduced himself and said that he had me as a biology instructor a few years back. He added that I was a very good and a hardworking teacher and that he enjoyed the class. My wife then asked how he had done in biology. He replied, "I dropped the class; it was too much work." I have since wondered about the kids who didn't drop and what they thought.

On the other side of the coin, I didn't let criticism get me down either—even though I listened to what students had to say. A few years ago, right after administering the first exam of the semester, I received a rude and somewhat nasty e-mail from an upper division student (the class was freshman level). The theme of the e-mail was that the exam was too hard, not fair, geared for graduate students not freshmen, etc. The note concluded with a comment that he did not like the way I talked down to him and to the rest of the class.

I replied that I was always glad to hear from students and to get their opinions, but I didn't like the tone of his message. The student was intelligent and did well in the class. In fact, he earned an A. I did not hear any more from him on a personal level, anyway. I sort of forgot the matter. However, when he handed in his final exam, he asked me if I was going to teach the class during summer session. When I asked why, he replied that his wife wanted to be in my class! Go figure.

Another reptile story, this one from ASU Mathematics Professor Dr. Betty L. Betty reported that several years ago she was doing a math workshop at the Catawba Science Center. When she arrived that morning, one of the museum's workers showed her to the room where she would be doing the workshop. The first thing she saw was a large snake curled up in its cage at one side of the room. When she mentioned that she was afraid of snakes (she is afraid of a fly and most living things) and would prefer not to be in that room, she was quickly assured it would not be a problem since the snake was securely locked in the wire cage. She stoically set up her teaching materials and started the activities when it came time for the workshop to begin. As she moved through the various activities of the morning session, she kept her eye glued on the snake. It seemed to be asleep and it never moved. By lunch, she was feeling a little more relaxed about teaching in a room with a snake. Afterward, she arrived back in the room and noticed several of the workshop participants standing around a metal wastebasket. She looked into the basket and to her horror, there was that snake looking her right in the eye. Needless to say, she hightailed it out of the room. After the folks at the Catawba Science Center returned the reptile to its cage, they finally persuaded her to come back in the room and continue the math workshop. To her credit, she did, but only while vowing that she will never again agree to teach in a room with a snake—even a little baby one.

One time I was helping a North Carolina seventh grade science class with an aquatic biology field trip. There were two female teachers in command of about 40 students. One of the teachers, Cynthia, was gung-ho for outdoor science activities; the other, Marge, not so much. While walking through the woods to the stream, Cynthia took me aside and advised me that Marge had her "panties in a wad." Now I am a northerner and was not familiar with that expression. I replied that there were several large trees on the trail and that I could distract the students while Marge got behind the trees and adjusted her undergarments. Cynthia gave me a look of disdain and stated that she had forgotten that I was not from around here.

On another field trip situation, this time involving a fifth grade class making inferences at the beach, the following occurred. The teacher, Alison, posed the question, "Why do you think the ocean water is so salty?" After several of the kids had offered ideas, one of the female class members said she had noticed several folks leaving pretzels and other salty morsels in the sand. She thought that the water from the sea would cover the salty foods at high tide and absorb the salt that way. (Must have been one heck of a lot of pretzels left at the beach.)

Some bad words . . .

The two following vignettes were offered by Mrs. P., a high school English as a Second Language (ESL) teacher in Northern Virginia. In the first case, a Middle Eastern boy and an Asian boy were arguing over some previous incident. One called the other a snitch for bringing it to Mrs. P.'s attention. The other boy, not being very fluent in English, said, "Mrs. P, he called me a bitch!"

The other incident came about when Mrs. P. said, "For this next assignment, I want each of you to take out two shits of paper." There was some laughing but Mrs. P. hoped that the incident would soon be forgotten. Two class periods later, a male student raised his hand. When the teacher recognized him, he playfully asked, "When are we going to do the assignment that requires two shits of paper?" News evidently travels fast in high schools—particularly when it is juicy. Another ESL story from Mrs. P.: One year she had a slightly older female high school student from Iraq enrolled in her class. The young lady was very attractive and also very quiet. Male class members tried to "hit" on her and frequently teased her and tried to get her attention. She said nothing. Unbeknown to the class and even to Mrs. P., the lovely young woman had married during a school break. When classes resumed, the teasing of the young woman began again. Finally, she turned to the guys who were the source of the teasing and loudly stated, "Leave me alone or I will have my husband beat you up." Teasing the young woman from Iraq was no longer a class problem.

In an effort to get the ESL students more familiar with English words and with numbers, Mrs. P.'s class would sometimes play Bingo. In one of the very first games, Mrs. P. had called out several numbers and noticed that the students had used most of the tokens, yet there had been no Bingos. She asked the students why no one had "Bingoed." Several students called out in unison, "When are you going to call 'free space?'" The lesson here: a teacher can never be too thorough with directions.

PAROCHIAL SCHOOL HUMOR

I include this section because of the reputation many Catholic schools have for discipline and maintaining order—from a nun's rap across the knuckles for a comma splice to a priest's boxing a young man's ears for forgetting to invert and multiply when dividing fractions. Mary S. from New York State still shudders when recounting how a nun berated her and a fourth grade friend for holding hands when reading a scary story. Mary and friend felt they were scarred for life just by trying to give comfort to one another.

On the other hand, a parochial school can sometimes act as a safe haven for its members. During Mary's first year of teaching, she was greeted one morning by drawings of middle fingers thrust through the loops of each draw-down curtain in the classroom. Mary calmly cut each digit out and claims that due to her protected childhood in a Catholic school and home, she did not know what

"giving the finger" meant.

Her husband, Fred, points out that the students weren't always angels, either. He recounts how during his sophomore year at an all-men's Catholic High School, a young wise guy popped off one time too many to the teacher priest. Father Whoever grabbed the lad by the collar and lifted him off the floor. The student was wearing suspenders, and Father hung the boy by the suspenders to the large wall hooks that held several large world and regional maps. The young man dangled there for the rest of the period, much to the delight of his classmates.

Fred also tells of the time that another young priest was assigned to teach Fred and some of his high school buddies. The young Father walked into a completely empty classroom. He ran back to the school office to see the older priest who served as the school principal. The students had removed all of the desks from the room and had placed them on the fire escape, along with themselves. When the two priests came back to the classroom, the students had already returned themselves and the desks to their appropriate positions and were sitting at attention smiling when the two instructors walked in. The younger priest felt extremely foolish, I am sure.

MORE RECENT STORIES

From Scott Taylor, a science teacher at Hibriten High School in Caldwell County, NC. I received this anecdote. Scott had an Honors Chemistry Class made up of a group of really bright kids. Most of them had parents that were professionals; doctors, lawyers, etc. This is the story of a day in which the students did a lab to determine the heat of fusion of ice. They used Styrofoam coffee cups for calorimeters, which were half-filled with ice. The students needed to heat some water to about 60 degrees C on a hot plate to use in the melting of the ice. A bright, young female student that ranked very high in her class did not read the procedures carefully. She put the water to be heated in the Styrofoam coffee cup and placed it on the hotplate to heat. The cup, of course, started to melt and made a terrible odor, making the entire room stink. She received a great deal of kidding over the incident, but learned the valuable lesson of reading procedures completely and understanding what needs to be done before starting a lab.

From Susan S. in Hamilton, Montana come the following kindergarten vignettes. One of my favorite kindergarten tales was the little wild boy who was having a bad day, and when I asked him why, he replied, "I guess I got up on the wrong side of my leg today."

One of her former students said she told her daughter that she was going to enroll her in school, and the child said, "Mom, instead of rolling me in, can we just walk in?"

And my friend's kindergarten grandson got in trouble for licking the projector. When his Dad asked him about it, he said, "I didn't lick the projector—I just wanted to see my tongue on the wall (overhead projector)." As I approach the end of the book and achieving closure, I am reminded of another story. Marianne L. of Richmond, Virginia tells this one by way of a related colleague. The colleague had a student teacher that particular school term and she asked Marianne's friend on how to achieve closure for a lesson. The colleague said, "Oh I just wait until about a minute before lunch time then I say, 'Kids look what time it is—hurry and line up to go eat.' That is how to achieve closure."

A final story comes from the world of drama. A good friend, Barbara R., was the head of the Drama Department at the University of Minnesota. Prior to that, she had plenty of acting experience. One night, while performing in the hit show *Guys and Dolls* at her school, Barbara was playing the role of Adelaide (the female lead who always had a cold). A particular scene had Adelaide reach into her bosom to draw out a lace-edged hanky on which to blow her nose. Unfortunately, when Barbara reached inside her dress, she pulled out a lace-edged "falsie" instead of a hanky. She proceeded to blow her nose on the garment and tucked it back under her dress. As no one knew better than Barbara, the show must go on.

My point is—humor is everywhere and usually you don't have to look very hard to find it. It can be very useful. In my own teaching experience I have used hundreds of silly sayings, jokes, and anecdotes—all to try to make a point or to get students of all ages to remember something they might not otherwise recall. Humor, of course, is important outside the academic setting. It can make a person feel better or dilute some criticism, or break the ice in an awkward social situation, and it can be utilized in parenting. As my grandmother used to say, in a rough situation it is better to laugh than to cry. Humor can also forge life-long relationships. My own matrimonial situation is a good example. Once, early on, while dating Dona, I asked her what she thought was the most important attribute about a guy that would make for a good husband. She immediately answered, "a good sense of humor." Yes, I thought! I do have a chance, after all, with this beautiful creature. I am certainly not mechanical-minded, rich, a good dancer or romancer, but one thing I do have is a sense of humor. I must have. She has been my wife for close to 50 years.

THE END

www.ingramcontent.com/pod-product-compliance
Ingram Content Group UK Ltd.
Pitfield, Milton Keynes, MK11 3LW, UK
UKHW022224230426
12048UKWH00016BA/1045